Healing Where It Hurts

Healing Where It Hurts

JAMES W. MOORE

DIMENSIONS
FOR LIVING

NASHVILLE

HEALING WHERE IT HURTS

93 94 95 96 97 98 99 00 01 02 — 10 9 8 7 6 5 4 3 2 1

This book is printed on acid-free, recycled paper.

Library of Congress Cataloging-in-Publication Data

Moore, James W. (James Wendell), 1938–
  Healing where it hurts/James W. Moore.
    p. cm.
  ISBN 0-687-16743-4 (alk. paper)
    1. Consolation. I. Title.
BV4905.2.M65 1993
248.8'6—dc20   92-45706

Most Scripture quotations are from the New Revised Standard Version Bible,
Copyright 1989 by the Division of Christian Education of the National
Council of the Churches of Christ in the USA. Used by permission.
  Those noted KJV are from the King James Version of the Bible.
  Some quotations are the author's own version.

With love
and appreciation for
our parents

Contents

CONTENTS

Introduction

*L*et me begin with three true stories. See if you can find the common thread that links them together.

• First, some months ago, I was watching a professional football game on television. The Houston Oilers were playing the Cincinnati Bengals in a very important conference game toward the end of the season.

The Oilers were having their problems. They could not stop Cincinnati's running attack. One of Houston's very best defensive players was limping noticeably, and he was being blocked and pushed around to the point that he was virtually ineffective. I had never seen him play so poorly.

Finally, the announcer said, "Well, he probably shouldn't even be out there. He is playing hurt. He has a stress fracture of the right leg and he just can't move. You can see how badly he's limping. He wants to play and he wants to win, but you can't do much with a fractured leg!"

• Not long after that, I was watching a videotape of the Boston Marathon. The camera came in tight on one of the runners. He, too, was limping dramatically. He is a world-class runner, but this was not his day, and eventually he had to drop out of the race.

The announcer explained: "He gave it the old college try, but he just couldn't compete today. He may have overtrained, because the incessant running and the constant pounding caused a stress fracture in his left foot and he had to drop out. The pain was too great."

• A few days later, I was visiting an older woman in her home. She has terminal bone cancer. She is being so courageous as she goes through this debilitating experience.

She said, "Jim, I have to move about very carefully because the cancer has so weakened my bones. At any moment, a sudden move or a wrong turn can cause a fracture." Even then, her arm was in a sling. The week before, she had fractured her right arm by the simple act of reaching over to pick up the telephone directory.

Of course, the common thread in the stories is the problem of *stress fractures*. There's an interesting thing to notice about stress fractures. They hobble us, but they do not prevent us from moving around. We walk, but we limp. We are in pain, but not totally immobilized. We go on with life, but not effectively. We are not completely broken, but we are dramatically cracked. We can't run and jump, but we can plod and trudge.

As I understand it, stress fractures can happen in three different ways—either from a hard blow, such as happened to that football player; from constant, continuous pounding, as with the marathoner; or from a deadly disease within that weakens the bones, as we see in the woman who is the victim of cancer.

Without question, physical stress fractures are painful and troublesome, but over the years I have come to realize that there is another kind of stress fracture that is even worse, even more painful, even more immobilizing, even more debilitating. Of course, I'm talking about the stress fractures of the spirit. When your spirit is cracked, your hopes are dashed, your dreams are shattered, and your heart is broken—there is nothing more crippling than that. Ironically, these spiritual stress fractures come in ways similar to the physical ones.

• Sometimes they are caused by a sudden hard blow—like the unexpected and tragic loss of a loved one, or the abrupt, shattering loss of a cherished dream.

• Or they may come from a constant incessant pounding—one disappointment after another, one hurt after another, one heartache after another, until we feel so defeated by life that the spring goes out of our step and we trudge listlessly along, thinking negative thoughts and seeing no real hope or joy anywhere.

• Still other spiritual stress fractures come from some emotional disease that has taken root deep down in our souls, working within to choke the life out of us. Hatred, prejudice, bitterness, and resentment are spiritual cancers that poison and paralyze and cripple us from within.

Do you know people who have spiritual handicaps? They walk, but they limp. They move, but they trudge. Zombie-like, they go through the motions, but inside, they have really quit on life. They are disillusioned. Life has turned sour for them. They feel hurt, forsaken, and let down. And so they limp through life, hobbled by a stress-fractured spirit. You know what I'm talking about, don't you? There are people all around us like that, so hurt by the blows of life that they just give up. We call them the walking wounded.

We see a dramatic picture of this in Luke 24. It is Easter afternoon. Cleopas and Simon had been followers of Jesus, but now they have thrown in the towel and are limping down the Emmaus Road like broken and defeated warriors. They know about the crucifixion. They saw it with their own eyes. But they do not yet know about the resurrection. They have not yet experienced the Risen Christ.

Disappointed, disillusioned, defeated, heartbroken, downcast, they trudge down the Emmaus Road toward home. Their hopes for the future have been dashed. Not knowing what else to do, they turn back toward the old life.

Picture them in your mind. Their shoulders are slumped. Their heads are bowed as though they carry on their backs a crushing burden of defeat and dejection. They limp along with weary steps, as if their shoes were weighted with lead. Their eyes are misted over with the tears of disillusionment. They walk along in silence. They dare not speak for fear they will break into uncontrollable sobbing.

At last, with a sigh weighted with despair, the younger man speaks: "He's dead. He's gone. It's all over. They have killed him and without him we are nothing. We should have known this wouldn't work. It was too good to be true, too idealistic for this cruel world. How could we have been such fools! We followed him. We trusted him. We thought he was the one to save us. And now it's all over."

Now, that is the bold portrait of the stress-fractured spirit—down, dejected, worn, weary, wounded. But we also know that that is not the end of the story. No! The Risen Lord comes to them. He walks with them. He talks with them. He opens the scriptures to them. He breaks bread with them—and as they experience the Resurrected Christ, look what happens. They, too, are resurrected! They are healed! They find new life! And they rush—no more trudging, no more limping—they *run* back to Jerusalem to share the good news with the other disciples.

Isn't that a great story? There are so many powerful

images and dramatic symbols here. It is packed full of the stuff of life. There are so many helpful lessons for us in this story. We could go in so many different directions. But for now, let me just lift up three special insights, three lessons which underscore the good news here—the good news for people who suffer from a stress-fractured spirit.

Lesson Number One: Christ Comes to Us in a Special Way When We Are Hurting

Christ is always with us in every circumstance of life, but over the years I have noticed that he seems to draw even closer to us when we are in pain. Cleopas and Simon were hurting that day as they plodded down the Emmaus Road. And then suddenly Christ was there with them to give them strength and meet their need. That's the way it works.

It seems that it would be easy for us to feel the presence of Christ with us when life is bright and beautiful and all the breaks are going our way, but the truth is that Christ is never nearer to us than when we are hurting. Time after time, I have heard people say it: "This is the hardest thing we have ever gone through. Our hearts are broken, but we will be all right because God is with us as never before." A hundred times or more, I have heard hurting people say that: "God is with us as never before."

He is uniquely and especially with us when we are hurting, and I think I know why. I think it's because God is like a loving father . . . who wants to be especially close to his children when they are in pain. Every parent knows what I'm talking about. Some months ago when our daughter suddenly became ill, we couldn't get there fast enough. We wanted to be with her. We wanted to help her. God is like that. This is an important lesson that explodes out of this story in Luke 24—Christ comes to us in a special way when we are hurting.

Lesson Number Two: Christ Has the Power to Heal Our Hurts

And in Luke 24, we see how it happens. Cleopas and Simon are trudging along with a stress-fractured spirit. But then Christ comes to them. He walks with them, symbolizing the importance of the daily walk with Christ. He talks with them, showing the power of prayer. He opens the scriptures to them, underscoring the importance of Bible reading. He breaks bread with them—an obvious plug for Holy Communion. And he sends them back to the church!

Don't you see? Prayer, Bible study, the sacraments, staying close to the church and the daily walk with Jesus Christ—through these holy habits, Christ can bring healing to a fractured spirit.

Lesson Number Three: Christ Shares His Resurrection with Us

When we experience the Risen Lord, we, like Cleopas and Simon, are resurrected too. We too receive new life.

I once heard a story about a first-grade schoolteacher who was having a horrible day. It had rained all day, and thirty-seven first-graders had been cooped up in a small classroom all day, with no recess. And the children were absolutely wild. She could not get them calmed down. There had been one problem after another all day long, and the teacher was beside herself, even more anxious than the children for the three o'clock bell to ring at the end of the school day.

At 2:45 the teacher noticed that it was still pouring outside, so she began the arduous task of getting the right raincoats, the right rainhats, and the right boots on the right children. Finally, she had all of them fixed and ready to go home, except for one little six-year-old boy. He had a pair of boots that were just impossible to get on. No zippers, no snaps, no hooks—they had to be pulled on with great effort.

The teacher pushed and pulled, yanked and jerked and tugged, until finally they slipped on, and she was so relieved.

But then the little boy said, "Teacher, you know what? These boots ain't mine!"

The teacher wanted to scream, but she didn't. She said a quick prayer, took a deep breath, pushed the hair back out of her face, and began the difficult process of getting the boots back off the little boy. She pulled and jerked and yanked and tugged, and finally they came off.

Then the little boy said: "They're my sister's, but she lets me wear 'em!"

The resurrection is not ours. It belongs to Christ, but he lets us wear it. And when we strap on the boots of Christ, when we take up his torch, when we commit ourselves to continue Christ's ministry of love, when in faith we accept him as our Savior—then we become whole, our stress fractures are healed, and we really come alive! This is the good news for us today: The Great Physician can revive us; he can bring healing where it hurts.

1.

When Life
Breaks Your Heart

II Corinthians 4:7-9 NRSV: But we have this treasure
in clay jars, so that it may be made clear that this
extraordinary power belongs to God and does not
come from us. We are afflicted in every way, but
not crushed; perplexed, but not driven to despair;
persecuted, but not forsaken; struck down, but not
destroyed.

Job 13:15a KJV: Though he slay me, yet will I trust
in him.

A few years ago, on one of the Monday-night
football telecasts, the sportscasters were dis-
cussing the great running backs of professional football
history. When they came to Walter Payton of the
Chicago Bears, they pointed out that he was the all-time
leading ground gainer in the National Football League.

Then Frank Gifford said, "What a runner! Do you
realize that all together, Walter Payton gained more than
nine miles rushing in his career? Just imagine that—
more than nine miles!"

To which the other sportscaster, Dan Dierdorff, responded, "And to think that every 4.6 yards of the way,
someone was knocking him down!"

Well, it happens not just in professional football. It's
true also in life. We do get knocked down a lot. The truth
is that every now and then, life will break our hearts!
And the question is, How do we respond to that? How

do we handle the defeats, the problems, the burdens, the knock-downs, the heartaches, the broken dreams?

The job you wanted and didn't get, the raise you needed that didn't materialize, the promotion that never came, the romance that fizzled and left you out in the cold, the business that looked so promising and then fell through, the child who got into trouble, the strained relationship with another person, the vicious gossip behind your back, the heart-wrenching problem in your marriage or family, the promising young man or woman who went off to fight a war in a foreign land and never came back, the accident that happened in the blink of an eye and changed your life forever, the dreaded news that you have a terminal illness—sickness, loneliness, financial problems, the death of a loved one, and I could go on and on—how do we handle all these problems?

There is no doubt about it—the broken heart is a real part of life. And as Christian people, the question we need to ask is not where did this heartache come from, but where does it lead? That is the question, and that is what the apostle Paul is underscoring in Second Corinthians when he expresses those powerful words of Christian faith and hope. He says that we "are afflicted in every way, but not crushed; perplexed, but not driven to despair; persecuted, but not forsaken; struck down, but not destroyed," because "we know that the one who raised the Lord Jesus will raise us also" and bring us into his presence. "So we do not lose heart." We are always of good courage.

Dealing with heartache and disappointment and suffering—that's also what the book of Job is about. Job was the wealthiest, the most influential, the most moral man in all the land. He was righteous, virtuous, a faithful servant of God. Job was a good man, one of the best. But then all of a sudden, tragedy struck. Suffering came upon Job in three distinct blows. First, he was stripped of his wealth. Then his children were destroyed. And third, he was inflicted with a painful disease.

Notice that all the problems we usually connect with tragedy had been put upon Job. Financial ruin; the grievous death of his children; a terrible, painful, debilitating illness—not to mention the whisperings of the neighbors about what horrible sins Job must have committed to bring the wrath of God down on him in such harsh fashion.

Of course we know that the neighbors were wrong. The suffering didn't come from God at all. It's helpful to remember what the psalmist said about this. He did not say, "My pain comes from the Lord" or "My tragedy comes from the Lord." No! He said, "My help comes from the Lord." The book of Job was written to show that God is not the source of our pain. Rather, God is the source of our strength and comfort.

But Job's neighbors didn't know that, so they whispered and gossiped and pointed their fingers. And Job had to live with the false accusations, the pain, the grief, the tragedy, the heartache.

What could Job do in that tragic situation? What can any of us do when suffering comes? It seems to me that there are three possible responses to trouble. Poetically speaking, we might put it like this: When life breaks our hearts, we have three choices:

• We can break down in self-pity;
• We can break out with resentment;
• Or we can break through with trust.

Let's take a look at these three possibilities.

We Can Break Down in Self-pity

We can just feel sorry for ourselves. We can throw in the towel and quit on life, and spend the rest of our days crying, "Woe is me!" Sadly, some people do just that. They choose the way of self-pity.

I could take you to the home of a woman I know who has chosen this option. She spends all day, every day, in the valley of self-pity. She gets up in the morning and goes to bed at night feeling sorry for herself. If I took you to see her, she would tell you in vivid detail all about her terrible plight. She would tell you about all the people who have done her wrong and all the problems life has thrust upon her—and she has quite a list.

Her mind operates now almost solely in the realm of self-pity, and that is so tragic! She has had some heart-breaking troubles, but haven't we all? Isn't it interesting to notice how that, as much as we dread tragedy and sorrow and suffering, we admire tremendously those who handle it well, those who refuse to give in to self-pity. In *Keeping First Things First*, John Gile warns us:

> Look out for self-pity. It is one of the most overlooked, powerful, devastating, clever, insidious forms of evil— because it is not recognized as evil. It gets past our guard, distorts reality. . . . Self-pity takes away our sense of humor, shuts down communication, and stifles our creative powers. It makes us concentrate on ourselves, miss the good we could be doing for others, and blocks out the voice of God. Letting all that happen to us is what makes self-pity so pitiful.

But this is indeed one option open to us, isn't it? We can choose this sad and pitiful way. When life breaks our hearts, we can break down in self-pity. I pray that we won't, but that is one possibility. Now look at another option.

We Can Break Out with Resentment

That's what Job's wife told him to do. "Just curse God and die," she said to him. Sadly, some people do indeed choose this way of resentment. They brood and seethe, and become more and more bitter with every passing day. There is no joy in their life, no hope, no gladness, only anger and hostility.

I could take you to the home of a man I know who lives almost exclusively now in the valley of resentment. He gets up in the morning and goes to bed at night mad at life. If I took you to see him today, as soon as he saw us, he would begin to give us the long list of his grievances. He is mad at the president. He is mad at the governor. He is mad at the mayor. He is mad at the church. He is mad at his neighbors and his in-laws. He is mad at everyone he meets. He's mad at the world. People dread to see him coming because he is so bitter and hostile and cynical—and that is so tragic!

He has not always been that way. I remember when he was a lot of fun, when he was creative and productive and happy. But no more. Now resentment is the controlling force in his life. He has had some major problems. He has had some bad things happen to him. He has experienced tragedy and suffering, to be sure, but haven't we all?

Please pay close attention for just a moment. This is so important! It is so important to realize that there is nothing in the world more devastating to your soul, nothing more debilitating to your spiritual life, than resentment! We need to avoid it like the plague!

But here again, it's an option open to us. I pray that we won't choose this sad and pitiful way when life knocks us down. But it is a choice we have. When life breaks our hearts, we can break down in self-pity or we can break out with resentment. Thank God there is another choice. We don't have to give in to self-pity or resentment. There is another option, a better way. When life breaks our hearts, there is a third choice.

We Can Break Through with Trust

This is the path Job ultimately took. Now, in all honesty, if you read the book carefully, you will see that Job did some of all three things. There's some self-pity there, and some resentment, too. They are there, but most of all, there is trust! He breaks through with trust! He says it so powerfully in chapter 13: "Though he slay me, yet will I trust in him" (13:15 KJV).

Some years ago, William Barclay faced a great tragedy. His twenty-one-year-old daughter and her fiance were both drowned in a tragic yachting accident. Just a few weeks before they were to be married, they were both killed.

Later, in his *Spiritual Autobiography*, Barclay wrote, "God did not stop that accident at sea, but He did still the storm in my own heart, so that somehow my wife and I came through that terrible time still on our own two feet." He continued, "The day my daughter was lost at sea, there was sorrow in the heart of God." Then he added this:

When things like that happen, there are just three things to be said. First, to understand them is impossible. Second, Jesus does not offer us solutions to them. What he does offer us is his strength and help somehow to accept what we cannot understand. Third, the one fatal reaction

21

is the bitter resentment which forever after meets life with a chip on the shoulder and a grudge against God. The one saving reaction is simply to go on living, to go on working, and to find in the presence of Jesus Christ the strength and courage to meet life with steady eyes. (pp. 45-46)

When we know that God is with us, nothing—not even death—can separate us from God and his love.

That's the good news of our faith—that as we accept God into our lives and commit our lives to him, nothing can separate us from God and his love and watchful care. No illness, no suffering, no misfortune, no disappointment, no tragedy—nothing, not even death, can cut us off from God's love. That's a good thing to know, a good thing to remember when heartache comes.

But here's the point. When life breaks our hearts, we have a decision to make. The choice is ours—we can break down in self-pity, we can break out with resentment, or, thank God, we can break through with trust.

2.

When the Ligaments of Love Are Strained

Colossians 3:14: Above all, clothe yourselves with love, which binds everything together in perfect harmony.

Col. 3:1-17

When studying the Scriptures, it is sometimes quite helpful and revealing to be able to go back and read the text in its original language. Often a word carries a meaning in the original that we can easily miss in our modern-day translations. For example, take the word *repent.* Many people would say that the word means "to feel sorry for your sins."

But the original Hebrew word in the Old Testament conveys a much deeper meaning. The original Hebrew word was *hashivenu,* and it does mean "to feel sorry for your sins," but it also was the word used in the military for the command "About face!" It means "turn around"; "don't go that way anymore"; "come back this way": "About face!"

The point is clear: To repent is to do more than just feel sorry for your sins. It means that you are so sorry for your sins that you want God to turn your whole life around. It means you've been going in the wrong direction and you want to change your ways. That's what *repent* means—*hashivenu!* About face! Turn around! Change your ways! Be born again!

Another example is found in the word *love.* In English, we only have one word to express that "many splendored thing," but the original Greek of the New Testament had many different and colorful words for love:

- *Eros,* which gives us our word *erotic,* was their word for sensual love.
- *Philia,* which gives us our word *philanthropy,* was their word for charitable, humanitarian love.
- *Storgé* was their word for family love.
- And *agapé* was their word for unconditional, sacrificial, self-giving love.

Now, the word *agapé* is a tremendously valuable word for us because it tells us so much about God. *Agapé* is the word used in the New Testament for God's love. The message is clear: God's love is unconditional, sacrificial, self-giving love. That's the way God loves us, and that's the way he wants us to love one another.

Still another example of the way the original words can be so helpful and revealing is found in the word *time.* The original Greek New Testament manuscripts used two completely different words for *time—chronos* and *kairos. Chronos,* which gives us our word *chronology,* is tick-tock time. It's empty time—humdrum, meaningless, boring, uneventful time—time measured by the ticking of the clock. Each second is exactly like the one that went before it and the one that will follow it. *Chronos* is drudgery time.

But thank God there is another kind of time. The Greeks called it *kairos. Kairos* time represents those rich, extra-special, dramatic moments when God breaks into our lives and reveals himself so powerfully that time seems to stand still—those crucial moments when God speaks loud and clear—and we are so wonderfully touched by the impact of that "kairos moment" that our lives are changed forever.

Now, notice that when Jesus came into Galilee preaching, he said, "The time is fulfilled and the kingdom of God is at hand." The word there in the Gospel of Mark is not *chronos*. It is *kairos*, because it was special time, crucial time, meaningful time, decisive time, God's time. No question about it—we can learn so much from these key words in the original languages of the Bible.

Recently I made a new discovery with regard to this that I found quite helpful. I was studying this magnificent passage from Colossians 3 in my Greek New Testament when I suddenly noticed something that somehow I had never seen before.

It has to do with the word *binds*. Paul says to the Colossians, and indeed to us: "Above all these, put on love, which binds everything together in perfect harmony" (3:14). Love binds all things together.

Now, here's what I noticed. The word *binds*, in the original Greek, is *sundesmos*. *Sundesmos* is also the word the Greeks used for *ligaments*. This is a tremendously important insight, especially when we couple it with the fact that Paul called the church the Body of Christ. The ligaments in the Body of Christ are made of love! Now, if you know anything at all about the human body, you know how important ligaments are:

• ligaments hold the body together;
• ligaments enable the body parts to work;
• ligaments give the body its ability to move and function;
• ligaments give power, direction, unity, coordination, and grace.

If you strain or tear or injure the ligaments, the body can't work right. Let me paraphrase Paul: "Above everything else, put on love because love 'ligaments' everything together in perfect harmony."

As I was studying this passage, my mind flashed back to my younger days when I was an athlete. And I remembered some of the injuries I sustained in sports:

• a sprained ankle playing football;
• a fractured foot playing basketball;
• a cleated leg playing baseball;
• a black eye playing soccer.

But, without question, the most debilitating and painful injury I ever experienced was a dislocated shoulder which strained the ligaments in my shoulder and arm. I was running track when I hit a hurdle going full speed and fell, dead weight, on my right shoulder and dislocated it. They popped my shoulder back into place immediately, but oh, those ligaments! They were so stretched and strained that my arm was absolutely useless for several weeks.

My shoulder, my arm, my elbow, my wrist, my hand, even my fingers, were affected. Nothing would work because the ligaments were damaged. They had to tape my arm up against my chest for a few days. And then I had to exercise and exercise and exercise to build up those ligaments. Only when the ligaments were exercised back into good shape—only then could my shoulder and arm and hand and fingers work again.

The apostle Paul loved sports, and he knew what he was talking about here. He knew how important the ligaments are in the human body, and he knew that the ligaments in the Body of Christ—the ligaments in the Body of the church—are made of love:

• if you strain the love, the Body won't work;
• if you tear the love, or neglect the love, or ignore the love, the Body of the church can't work;

• if the ligaments of love are in good shape, the church can do amazing, incredible things; but
• if the ligaments of love are out of whack, the church is absolutely paralyzed, crippled, useless.

Now let's take this analogy a little further and break it down a bit.

The Ligaments of Love Bind Us Together

William Barclay put it like this: "Love is the binding power which holds the whole Christian body together. The tendency of any body of people is sooner or later to fly apart; and love is the one bond which will hold them together in unbreakable fellowship."

Our son, Jeff, knows first-hand about the significance of ligaments. He has undergone surgery on his knees because of ligament damage from football injuries. We have a videotape of the game in which he was hurt that first time. We can hardly bear to watch it, because as his teammates are carrying him off the field, his right leg is flopping and dangling as if disconnected from the rest of his body. We should have known then (it was a sure sign) that the ligaments were torn. Through the miracle of modern medicine, the doctors were able to make him some new ligaments, and if you saw him now, you would never know he had endured this problem. They reattached him.

That's what love does. It binds us together, joins us together, holds us together. It "ligaments" us together. In *The Different Drum*, M. Scott Peck tells a rather poignant and mysterious story that speaks to this. It's called "The Rabbi's Gift."

The story concerns a monastery that had fallen on hard times. There were only five monks left—all of them over seventy years of age. In the woods near the monastery was a hut visited from time to time by a rabbi from a nearby town. One day, in desperation, the abbot went to the rabbi to ask if he had any advice for their dying monastery.

The rabbi said, "I have no advice to give really. The only thing I can tell you is that one of you could well be the Messiah."

When the old abbot returned to the monastery, the other four monks gathered around him: "Well, what did the rabbi say? Did he have good counsel for us?"

"No, he couldn't help," the abbot answered. "We just wept and prayed and read the Scriptures together. The only thing he did say, just as I was leaving, was something rather cryptic. He said that one of us might be the Messiah. I don't know what he meant by that."

In the months that followed, the old monks pondered the rabbi's words. The Messiah? One of us? But if that is so, which one?

• Do you suppose he meant the Abbot? Yes, if he meant anyone, surely it's Father Abbot.
• On the other hand, maybe he meant Brother Thomas. Thomas is a holy man.
• Certainly he could not have meant Brother James. James gets rather crotchety at times. But he is virtually always right.
• But surely not Brother Phillip. Phillip is so passive—and yet somehow he is always there when you need him.

As they contemplated, the old monks began to treat one another with extraordinary love and respect—on the off-chance that one of them might be the Messiah.

Because the forest was really quite beautiful, people would come there to picnic and play. Occasionally, some of them would enter the old monastery, and they began to sense the extraordinary love and respect that now surrounded the five old monks—love that bound them together and radiated from them, permeating the atmosphere. The people told their friends, and they came and brought others.

Soon some of the younger men asked if they could join the monks. And then others joined. So within a few years, the once-dying monastery had come to life as never before. It became a thriving order and, thanks to the Rabbi's Gift, a vibrant center of light and spirituality.

Now, what is the meaning of that story? Simply this—when we treat one another with love and respect, the kind of love and respect we would give to Christ, then it not only binds us together but binds other people to Christ. It draws other people to Christ like an irresistible magnet. The ligaments of love bind us together.

The Ligaments of Love Enable Us to Move

Just as the ligaments in our human bodies enable us to move and function, so the ligaments of love give us the strength and coordination to live and move spiritually.

A friend recently told me the story of Fanniedell Peeples. Fanniedell Peeples is a volunteer at Children's Hospital of Michigan in Detroit. Fanniedell is very poor and nearly seventy years of age.

She has suffered from severe curvature of the spine since she was a small child. And she was teased every day of her childhood. But one day she discovered something—that her pain seemed to vanish when she was helping other people. When she reached out in love to others, her suffering went away, and in its place there came a warm glow.

So she has devoted her life to helping the families who come to Children's Hospital. She is an inspiration to both the staff and the patients, who marvel at her spirit and perseverance.

Interestingly, she admits that every night when she goes home to her empty, cold house, the pain and loneliness return. But she gets out of bed every morning and finds meaning and joy and purpose in loving and helping others. Love motivates her. Love keeps her going. Love enables her to function. Love empowers her.

The ligaments of love bind us together; the ligaments of love enable us to move.

The Ligaments of Love Work Best When Exercised

Recently I saw a movie on television called *The Dead Zone*. It's about a man who has a terrible car wreck, and as a result goes into a deep coma for five years. When he first comes out of the coma, he can't walk. You know why, don't you? Because the ligaments in his legs had not been exercised for five years. The ligaments had shrunk and debilitated because of lack of exercise.

Well, the message there for us is obvious. Just as body ligaments need exercise to be effective, so do the ligaments of love. They work best when used and exercised. You see, it's not enough to feel love; we need to exercise it, act it out, do it.

During the Los Angeles riots, an amazing act of love took place. A Hispanic, Fidel Lopez, had been jerked out of his truck and beaten senseless by the rioters. He was being hit mercilessly with sticks and bats and bottles. He was being kicked repeatedly and battered with angry fists. A crowd of people stood by and watched.

Suddenly an African American minister, the Reverend Bennie Newton, came on the scene. Immediately, he ran, diving and covering Lopez's body with his own. He screamed at the wild-eyed mob, "Stop it! Kill him and you'll have to kill me, too!'"

Bennie Newton turned back the rioters, and then he picked up the unconscious man and drove him to Daniel Freeman Hospital. Later, the Reverend Newton took up a collection at his church to repay Fidel Lopez the $3,000 the looters had stolen from him that afternoon.

Some days later, the two men met. They hugged each other and cried.

Fidel Lopez said to Reverend Newton, "How can I ever thank you? You saved my life! But why? Why did you do it? Why did you risk it?"

Newton said, "Because I am a Christian. I believe in sowing love, not hate. I believe in helping, not hurting. I believe in Jesus Christ, the Prince of peace and love."

The Reverend Bennie Newton obviously practices what he preaches, and he obviously knows that the ligaments of love bind us together. They enable us to move, and they work best when exercised.

3.

When You Are Fighting a Virus in Your Soul

~~~

1-4 *Matthew 6:1-2:* Beware of practicing your piety before others in order to be seen by them: for then you have no reward from your Father in heaven.

So whenever you give alms, do not sound a trumpet before you, as the hypocrites do in the synagogues and in the streets.

43-48 *Matthew 5:43-44:* You have heard that it was said, "You shall love your neighbor and hate your enemy." But I say to you, Love your enemies and pray for those who persecute you.

25-34 *Matthew 6:25, 33:* Therefore I tell you, do not worry about your life . . . . But strive first for the kingdom of God and his righteousness, and all these things will be given to you as well.

*H*ave you heard the old story about the wife who became concerned about her husband's health? He was a physical wreck, weak and pale and flabby, stressed out, and constantly tired—totally out of shape. So she took him to the doctor for a check-up.

When the examination was completed, the doctor came out to the waiting room and said to the wife, "Thelma, I just don't like the way your husband looks."

She said, "Neither do I, but he is good to the children!"

Now, believe it or not, there is a point to that story, and here it is: The inner life is more important than outward appearance.

Jesus believed that. He talked about that a lot. He was

~~~

supremely interested in the inner life. The Great Physician was vastly interested in the health of our souls.

In fact, he was so concerned about it that his toughest words were spoken to those who looked good outwardly but were sick within: "Woe to you, scribes and Pharisees . . . for you are like whitewashed tombs, which outwardly appear beautiful, but within they are full of dead men's bones" (Matt. 23:27). These are stark words.

He also said: "Woe to you, scribes and Pharisees . . . for you cleanse the outside of the cup and the plate, but inside you are full of greed and wickedness." Hard words!

And, "Beware of false prophets who come to you in sheep's clothing, but inwardly are ravenous wolves." Again, firm words.

Well, what are we to make of this? Why did Jesus speak so strongly about this? Well, it's because he realized that the single most destructive disease, the single most devastating illness, is the sickness within—the sickness in the soul. A hymn writer who understood the importance of this once wrote these words: "It is well with my soul." Can you say that? Is it well with your soul? Is your soul alive and well and close to God? Or is your soul sick and in need of healing?

Throughout the Sermon on the Mount, Jesus exposes a number of the more dangerous spiritual viruses that can so quickly invade and infect and poison our souls. Now I would like to take a look at a few of these destructive diseases that can so easily sneak up on us and make us the victims of soul sickness. Here is the first one.

Pride Is a Sickness of the Soul

Pride is a spiritual virus that will devastate your soul. Now, let me hurry to say that there is a good kind of pride. We all know that. It's good to be a proud American. It's good to be proud of your state, your school, your church, your heritage, your family.

But that's not the kind of pride Jesus is talking about in the Sermon on the Mount. He is exposing here that unhealthy pride, pride that is arrogant and pompous and haughty. The holier-than-thou pride—pride that shouts to the world "I'm better than you," pride that is conceited, pretentious, and puffed-up. That kind of pride is so dangerous and so destructive—and it will so quickly poison your soul.

Remember how Jesus put it: "Beware of practicing your piety before men in order to be seen by them." And, "When you give alms, sound no trumpet before you." And, "When you pray do not show off. Do not stand on street corners offering up empty phrases, trying to impress people with your many words."

Jesus had chosen for himself the way of the suffering servant, the humble, self-giving Savior, and therefore he would not be impressed with "religious show-offs." He saw that kind of arrogant pride as a dramatic symbol of "soul sickness."

One of Aesop's fables makes the point. It's the one about the group of mice that decided they needed to be better organized. So they elected some leaders. For awhile, all went well. The leaders were helpful and effective in devising innovative ways to find food and creative ways to escape from the house cat. And all in the mouse kingdom were happy.

But then as time went along, the mice leaders became more and more caught up in their own self-importance. They said, "We are the leaders here. We should have titles and special privileges. We should wear handsome uniforms with lots of medals, and tall hats, so everyone will recognize us immediately when we pass by and give us the proper respect."

So they did just that. They put on their uniforms and medals and tall hats—and they looked so good and felt so proud.

But then one day the cat launched a surprise attack! All the mice ran for their lives. But the mice leaders were so weighted down by their numerous heavy medals that they couldn't run fast. But even worse, when they reached the escape hatch, they couldn't get in because their hats were too tall! And the hungry cat had a sumptuous feast that day! The puffed-up mice leaders were destroyed by their own vanity and pride.

Within this story is the same message Jesus was underscoring in the Sermon on the Mount—namely this: Arrogant pride is dangerous; haughty pride is destructive; pompous pride is a spiritual virus that will devastate your soul.

The antidote for the disease of pride is a healthy dose of humility. But the point is clear: The disease of selfish pride can make your soul sick. We need to avoid it like the plague!

Hate Is Another Symbol of Sickness in the Soul

Someone hurts you or ignores you or slights you or becomes a threat to you—and you resent it! You want to lash out and get even. You hold a grudge, and hatred "burns deep" within you. I don't know anything more spiritually depleting than that. Someone has called it ill will, and that says it all. It is indeed sick.

Some years ago, Dr. Albert Beaven of Rochester told a story about something that happened to him when he was in college. One of his classmates did something that hurt him, and it made Albert Beaven so mad that he was determined to get even. So he picked up a sticky burr that had fallen from a tree on campus and put it in his pocket. The burr was covered with sharp, porcupine-like thorns. The plan was to carry the burr until he saw that fellow who had done him wrong. He wanted to throw it at him or rub it on his back.

All day long he kept that burr in his pocket, just waiting for his chance. Every time he took a step, the burr stuck in his leg. Every time he sat down, it hurt even more. Finally at the end of the day, he pulled the burr from his pocket and realized that all the thorns were gone. They were all sticking in him!

Hate is like that. It hurts us more than the people toward whom it's directed. Psychologists will tell you that every day, people are digging their own graves with their hateful grudges. The miracle prescription here to knock out the virus of hate is a healthy dose of Christian love. My friend Myrtle Day expressed it beautifully in her poem "Spiritual Healing":

> I could not wish for any fuller joy
> Than to be filled with the nature of my Lord,
> That His Spirit possess my being,
> That His perfect love shine in my life.
> That His gift of peace be cradled in my heart
> Then shall all striving cease
> Burdens, lightly borne
> Then shall my body, mind and spirit be
> Completely whole and free.

There is no question about it—pride and hate are dangerous and destructive. They are spiritual viruses that will infect and poison your soul.

Finally, There Is the Spiritual Virus of Worry

Worry, fretfulness, anxiety—whatever you want to call it—is yet another spiritual disease that will lead to soul sickness.

Broadly speaking, there are two kinds of anxiety. One, creative worry, is necessary; the other, silly, useless fretting, is destructive. The truth is that we can't stop worrying, because God has put within us, for our own good, a certain amount of worry energy, or anxiety energy. It's part of our basic make-up, and it's there for good reason.

So the question is not, Will we worry? We will! We can count on that. The question is, How do we use our worry energy creatively? How do we use our worry energy productively? How do we let our anxiety energy work for us rather than against us? The problem is not that we worry, it's that many of us do not know how to put our worries to work or how to use this anxiety energy for good.

If we never worried about our children, we would be terrible parents. If we had no concern for our nation or our city, we would be awful citizens. If we never worried about our jobs or had no consideration for a job well-done, we would be pitiful workers. If we had absolutely no concern for our church, we would be pathetic church members. If we never worried about making ends meet, we would be in big trouble!

So the key is to learn how to distinguish between creative worry and silly fretting. There is a big difference between the two. Creative worry spurs us to action; silly fretting completely paralyzes us. Creative worry causes us to stand tall for what is right; silly fretting pushes us deep down into self-pity.

In the Sermon on the Mount in Matthew 6, when Jesus says, "Do not be anxious," he is not talking about creative worry. He is not talking about thoughtful consideration or loving concern or careful, sensible planning. Rather, he's talking about silly, useless, immature fretting. Someone expressed it in a poem called *The Worry Cow*, which goes like this:

> The worry cow would have lived till now
> If she hadn't lost her breath.
> But she thought her hay wouldn't last all day
> So she mooed herself to death!

That kind of worry can kill. It's a spiritual virus that invades and infects and poisons our souls. It robs us of our vitality and poise and the ability to think straight. It makes emotional wrecks of us, takes away the radiance of living, and makes us mere skeletons of our real selves.

In Matthew 6, Jesus actually gives us a magnificent solution to the problem of worry—a threefold prescription, a threefold antidote:

- First, trust God completely;
- Second, make God the King of your life;
- Third, live one day at a time.

Some years ago, a young man named George Matheson entered Glasgow University. He had a keen mind. His hopes were high. Soon he and his fiancee would be married. He dreamed of a bright future. But suddenly the bottom dropped out—he became totally blind! Then because of his misfortune, he was rejected by his fiancee. She said she couldn't marry a blind man, and she left him. His world crumbled at his feet. Devastated, afraid, worried, he turned to God as never before—and God was there!

Struck blind, hurt, and rejected, George Matheson reached out in the darkness and found that God's love is always there for us. And then he sat down and wrote what has become one of our most beloved hymns—a hymn sung by Christians everywhere that says it all, a hymn of praise to God:

> O Love that wilt not let me go,
> I rest my weary soul in thee;
> I give thee back the life I owe,
> that in thine ocean depths its flow
> may richer, fuller be.

That is the answer to the problem of worry—the "blessed assurance" that no matter what difficulties we have to face, God will always be there for us and will see us through. We can claim that promise, and we can live in that confidence.

How is it with your soul? Are you suffering from soul sickness? If so, let me tell you something: There is a doctor in the house! The Great Physician is here for you. If you will let him, he can touch you and make you whole. He can perform a miracle of healing for you. He can turn your pride into humility, your hate into love, and your worry into confidence.

4.

When You Are Heading for a Breakdown

II Corinthians 13:~~5-11~~: Examine yourselves to
see whether you are living in the faith. Test
yourselves. Do you not realize that Jesus Christ is
in you?—unless, indeed, you fail to meet the
test! . . . Finally, brothers and sisters, farewell. Put
things in order, listen to my appeal, agree with one
another, live in peace; and the God of love and
peace will be with you.

13 -

ate on a Sunday night as I was rummaging
around in my office at home, I ran across an old
newspaper article, yellow with age, that I had clipped
out and saved for several years. It was from the sports
pages of the *New York Times,* and the dateline was
Knoxville, Tennessee, October 31, 1976.

The story was about Coach Ray Mears, the basketball
coach at the University of Tennessee at that time. It was
announced that Coach Mears was taking a leave of
absence from his coaching duties because of nervous
exhaustion. Some thirteen years earlier, in 1963, Coach
Mears had suffered a nervous breakdown, and from that
experience, he had learned how to recognize the danger
signs, the red flags that would warn him that he was
heading for trouble.

Now, here is the part of the article that caught my attention. A university spokesman said, "It's important to note

that this is not a nervous breakdown. From what we understand, he had gone through all this before. This time, he knew all the symptoms and notified the right people before the problem became too serious. He got medical help before it was too late."

He recognized the symptoms. He saw what was happening in his life, and he got help before he had a complete nervous breakdown. A short time later the coach came back and led his team to a winning season. Now it occurred to me as I read that statement that this can happen to us in our spiritual lives. We can have a spiritual breakdown! However, there are recognizable symptoms—red flags, caution lights, warning signals—that tell us clearly that we may be heading toward a spiritual breakdown.

That is precisely what the apostle Paul is telling the Corinthian Christians in II Corinthians 13. In effect, he is saying to them and to us that if you don't live as God wants you to live, certain things will happen to give you warning that you are drifting away from God, that you are neglecting the faith and heading toward a spiritual breakdown. And my, how the Corinthians needed to hear that! Their church was literally being torn apart by selfishness, jealousy, immorality, hostility, hatred, all kinds of problems. In the Corinthian letters, Paul is writing to a troubled and divided church—divided by factions and changes; divided by immoral destructive conduct; divided by lawsuits among the members.

Let me give you just one graphic example to show you how bad off and mixed up the Corinthian church had become. You remember that in the early church, Holy Communion—The Lord's Supper—was a full meal. It was a time when the church came together as a family, to celebrate God's love for them and their love for God and

41

one another; to celebrate God's goodness and generosity, and their unity and harmony as his children. But look what had happened at Corinth. After Paul left them, they got so far off the track, it was unbelievable. Holy Communion wasn't holy in Corinth! It had become a spiteful, ugly battleground. Some members would rush to communion and purposely try to eat all the food, so the latecomers (who weren't in their group) wouldn't get anything to eat! This was their cruel way of treating those they didn't like!

That's a sick spirit, isn't it! It is the opposite of Holy Communion, the opposite of what the Lord's Supper is all about. Now when Paul heard what was going on, he became angry! He wrote a series of letters to try to straighten them out. Of course, the crown, the high point, the mountaintop of that writing, is found in I Corinthians 13, the "love chapter." Paul has spent twelve chapters exposing their sinful ways, their red flags, their danger signs, and then in chapter 13, he says, "Now then, I will show you a better way." And he proceeds to tell them that the way to stay healthy as a Christian, the way to live the Christian life, is to live the life of love, and that the ethical question the Christian asks is, What is the loving thing to do?

But then at the end of these letters to the Corinthians, Paul says to them, "Examine yourselves to see whether you are living in the faith." That is, *be on guard!* Watch for the warning signals!

Now, the questions for us are: What are the red flags? What are the danger signs? What are the symptoms that warn us we may be heading for a spiritual breakdown? There are many. Let me propose three, and I'm sure you will think of others. But for now, let me invite you to take a look at these.

When It's Hard to Say Yes to Life

When we become negative, irritable, cynical, ungrateful, pessimistic, caustic—when we constantly feel sorry for ourselves, when we say no to life, rather than yes—that is the surefire warning signal that we are drifting away from God and heading for spiritual trouble. God created life in this world and called it good. Jesus came that we might live meaningfully and abundantly. As Christians, we are called to say yes to life, to affirm life, to celebrate life—to live with zest and gratitude, with enthusiasm and exuberance—and when we fail at that, that is God's warning signal that we are backsliding.

In *The Vital Balance,* Karl Menninger describes negative people as "rigid, chronically unhappy individuals, bitter, insecure and often suicidal." And then he goes on to underscore the importance of the positive personality by telling a beautiful story about Thomas Jefferson that came out of the early days of the settling of our country.

When Thomas Jefferson was president of our nation, he came one day with a group of friends to a swollen river. They were on horseback, riding cross-country. At the river bank was a hitchhiker, a man on foot who couldn't get across the swollen stream. He was standing there trying to catch a ride, trying to find somebody who would transport him across the river.

When President Jefferson and his party rode up, this hitchhiker went straight over to the President and asked for a ride across the stream. Jefferson reached down, grabbed him by the arm, and pulled him up on the horse behind him. Together they forded the stream and he then let him off on the other side.

An onlooker came over and, with an amazed look, said to the hitchhiker, "Out of all those men, why in the world did you ask the president to bring you across the river?"

The man answered, "I didn't know he was the president. I just knew he had a 'yes' face!"

The Bible tells us again and again that God has a "yes" face, and he wants us to say yes to life. I find in my own life that when I begin to harbor negative feelings, it is a red flag, a warning signal, that I am getting away from God and losing faith, heading for a spiritual breakdown.

When It's Hard to Say Yes to Other People

When we feel out of sorts with other folks, when we feel like everybody is against us and out to get us, when we feel as if we want to withdraw or hide or run away from people, when we feel hostile toward others and want to criticize or attack or hurt them—that too is a surefire sign that we are drifting away from God.

The scriptures make it very clear that there is a strong relationship between our faith and the way we feel toward other people and relate to them. God made us out of love and for love, and when we have trouble loving and accepting other folks, it is a symptom of spiritual sickness.

In the Sermon on the Mount, Jesus says, "If you are offering your gift at the altar and there remember that someone has something against you, go first and be reconciled and set that right, and then come back to the altar and make your gift." The point is clear and significant. We cannot come into the presence of God with hatred or resentment in our hearts!

Dr. Carl Rogers, a noted psychologist from La Jolla, California, made a profound statement that is worth sharing:

44

I have come to believe that appreciating individuals is rather rare. I have come to think that one of the most satisfying experiences I know—and also one of the most growth-promoting experiences for the other person—is just to fully appreciate an individual in the same way I appreciate a sunset. . . . People are just as wonderful as sunsets—if I can let them be.

But, if I look at a sunset, as I did the other evening, I do not find myself saying, soften the orange a little on the right-hand corner, and put a bit more purple along the base, and use a little more pink in the cloud cover. I don't do that. I watch it with awe, as it unfolds. It's best when I can experience others in this way—just appreciating the unfolding of a life. Not attacking. Not criticizing. Not correcting . . . just appreciating others like we appreciate and enjoy the wonder, the beauty, and the uniqueness of a sunset.

There is nothing more emblematic of the Christian faith than love, and when we drift away from that, we drift away from God.

When It's Hard to Say Yes to God

We may be heading toward a "spiritual breakdown" when we have difficulty praying or studying the scriptures or making it to church; when we have trouble doing God's will or trusting God, being grateful to God or inspired by God—these are all clear symptoms of "soul sickness."

There is a story often told about Coach "Bear" Bryant. When Bryant was the football coach at Alabama, his team was winning an important game by four points! But in the fourth quarter, with only forty seconds left in the game, the Alabama quarterback was hurt and had to be helped off the field.

Coach Bryant called for his second-string quarterback and said to him, "Now, son, we have a four-point lead with forty seconds left. I want you to get in there and run out the clock. Don't hand the ball off. Don't pass the ball. Just roll out to the right, run off as much time as you can, and when you sense you are about to be tackled, just go down and hang on to the ball."

With those instructions, the young quarterback ran into the game. He called the play, took the snap, and rolled out to his right. But then he saw his wide receiver wide open down field, and the quarterback thought to himself, "I've never completed a pass in a college game." And he couldn't resist the temptation. So he threw it! But just as he was letting it go, he was hit from behind and the ball squirted up in the air.

It was intercepted by the fastest cornerback in the Southeastern Conference, who started swiftly down the sideline for what could be the winning touchdown for the other team. But suddenly, the Alabama quarterback who had thrown the errant pass (against Coach Bryant's instructions) got up and started to chase the speedy cornerback. Unbelievably, incredibly, miraculously, he caught him and tackled him at the five-yard line, just as the horn sounded. Alabama had won the game—much to the relief of the quarterback.

After the game, the other coach congratulated Coach Bryant: "I can't believe your quarterback caught my man. He is one of the fastest runners in the United States. I don't know how in the world he caught him."

"Well, it's really very simple," said Coach Bryant. "Your man was running for a touchdown. My man was running for his life!" It's amazing what you can do when you are properly motivated!

Now, if a young football player can be that powerfully motivated by fear of his coach, why can't we turn the coin over and be that powerfully motivated by our confidence in God, our trust in God, our faith in God? Many years ago, Isaiah sensed the presence of God in the Temple.

God said to him, "There are problems in the land and I need a prophet for this hour. I need someone to serve me . . . and speak out for me."

And Isaiah answered, "Yes! Here am I, Lord!"

Can you say yes to God like that—"Yes, Lord. Here am I, send me"? The apostle Paul reminds us: "Examine yourselves to see whether you are living in the faith." Well, how about it? Can you say yes to life? Can you say yes to other people? Can you say yes to God? If so, you can be spiritually healthy and whole, and you can have the joyful, meaningful, abundant life that God wants to give you.

5.

When You Need a Life-changing Moment

1 - 10

Luke 19:2-5, 8-9. A man was there named Zacchaeus; he was a chief tax collector and was rich. He was trying to see who Jesus was, but on account of the crowd he could not because he was short in stature. So he ran ahead and climbed a sycamore tree to see him, because he was going to pass that way. When Jesus came to the place, he looked up and said to him, "Zacchaeus, hurry and come down; for I must stay at your house today."

Zacchaeus stood there and said to the Lord, "Look, half of my possessions, Lord, I will give to the poor; and if I have defrauded anyone of anything, I will pay back four times as much." Then Jesus said to him, "Today salvation has come to this house."

A good friend of mine had a traumatic experience a couple of summers ago that dramatically changed his life. John was on vacation with his family on the Atlantic coast near Savannah, Georgia, when it happened. Swimming alone one day at high tide, he was hit by a huge wave and knocked unconscious for a few moments. When he came to a bit, he realized that he was face down, under water.

The force of the wave had knocked him in toward the shoreline, and the water there was not very deep, but he was paralyzed. It turned out to be a temporary paralysis, but he didn't know that at the time. He only knew that he was face down, under water, and unable to move. Can you imagine that?

John thought to himself, "This is it! This is how it all ends for me! I'm going to die! I'm going to drown right here in the shallow waters of the Atlantic Ocean!"

Later, as he reflected on that moment, he remembered that he felt remarkably calm, and he had two thoughts. Today, he smiles about that and says, "Most people at a time like that would have more than two thoughts, but I've led a very dull life, so only two images came to mind."

First he thought, "My wife doesn't deserve this!" They had just gone through the horrendous experience of nursing their twenty-year-old son through the consequences of a terrible motorcycle accident which almost took his life, an accident that required extensive surgery and months of therapy and tender loving care. They were just coming out of that agonizing ordeal, and now here was John, lying paralyzed under water in the ocean and thinking, "Jane doesn't deserve this."

His second thought was, "I've got a big job with lots of authority and clout and prestige, and I'm going to die here in the waters of the Atlantic Ocean. Somebody's going to get my job, and others will get nice promotions because of my loss. I'm creating slack in the job market!"

Just about then, a little boy playing in the surf stepped on John. The young boy ran to get his parents: "Mom! Dad! Come quick and help me! There's a man drowning down there!"

Well, the initial reaction of the parents was (How shall I say this?) parental! They were resting and reading under their beach umbrella and didn't want to be bothered. They didn't believe the little boy. They tried to dismiss him with a wave of the hand: "Now Billy, that imagination of yours! Nobody's drowning. Go on and play. Don't disturb us. Go play in the water or build a sand castle."

But bless little Billy's heart! He would not be put off. He urgently grabbed his parents by their hands and literally pulled them down to where the surf was pounding against the beach and John was drowning. Billy and his parents pulled John out of the water and the mother ran for help.

Later John would say, "What a message! I was saved by the love and concern of a little child. A little child shall lead them." The lifeguard administered CPR and revived John.

"As I came back to consciousness," John said, "I remember hearing voices as if they were way off in the distance, repeating something over and over. Then I heard the lifeguard saying, 'John, can you hear me? John, can you hear me?'"

John was rushed to the hospital. He was in intensive care and on life-support for several days. But now, because of the active, persistent love of a six-year-old boy; because of the expert work of a well-trained lifeguard; because of the commitment and diligence and wisdom of good doctors and nurses; because of the love, support, and prayers of his family and friends; and because of the miracle of God's grace and his healing touch, John is alive and well, active and healthy!

Now, let me tell you something interesting. If John were here with us today, he would say something that would at first sound startling. He would say, "I wish that wave had hit me thirty years ago, because that traumatic experience, horrible as it was, changed me! Strange as this may sound, it was the best thing that ever happened to me. It changed my life! It changed my values, my commitments, my concerns. It changed my priorities—and did they ever need changing! It drew me closer to my family. It taught me how to celebrate the preciousness of life. It brought me closer to God! Yes, I wish that wave had hit me thirty years ago!"

Now, why would John say that? For one reason and one reason only—because it was a life-changing moment. Let me ask you, How long has it been since you had a life-changing moment? A moment that touched you so profoundly, so powerfully, so deeply that you could never be the same again—a life-changing moment. Isn't that precisely what the Zacchaeus story in Luke 19 is all about? Isn't that what happened to Zacchaeus? He was changed, redeemed, converted, saved, turned around. Christ came into his life and made him over!

Somewhere back in the past, Zacchaeus had gotten off the track. The children sing "Zacchaeus was a 'wee little man.' " Well, he was a "wee little man" all right, not only in physical stature, but also in spirit. Bad habits had taken root in him—greed, selfishness, the lust for power, prestige, and money. And they were destroying him, cutting him off from other people and from God.

But then Jesus came into his life, and look what happened to Zacchaeus. We see in his experience the drama of redemption, the power of conversion, the miracle of the life-changing moment. When the light of Christ spilled into his life, Zacchaeus was exposed in all his littleness. He saw himself. Perhaps for the first time, he saw himself as he really was—greedy, self-centered, a traitor, a cheat, a con man. And Zacchaeus didn't like what he saw. He was ashamed and penitent. But he realized that help was available. Even after all he had done, he felt somehow that this man from Nazareth could help him. And he changed. Talk about a conversion! By the miracle of grace, through the presence and love of Christ, his life was changed! Christ came into his life and made him over.

Don't miss the impact of this. Don't miss the message for your life now. If you are doing something you ought not to be doing; if you are possessed by some bad habit that is tearing you apart; if you are living a life-style you are ashamed of; if you have somehow gotten away from God and the church; if you want to change, God has a life-changing moment for you. If, in faith, you will trust him and turn it over to him, he will turn your life around! He can bring healing where it hurts. Look at Zacchaeus again, and notice how completely he was changed when Christ came into his life.

Zacchaeus Was Changed Personally

Zacchaeus got a new view of himself because Jesus called him by name. Everybody else in town had labeled Zacchaeus, and the labels they attached to him were not attractive, but Jesus walked up and called him by name: "Zacchaeus, come down. Zacchaeus, I choose to have lunch with you." I love that because I know how dangerous, how destructive, and how painful labels can be.

When I was twelve years old, one of my school buddies slipped a pack of Lucky Strikes out of the glove compartment of his dad's car. He promptly lit one up and he offered me one. And when I said no, he called me "yellow-backed scaredy cat." Now, that was a life-changing moment for me! From that moment, I never have liked labels!

Another occasion when the label didn't fit me was the time I spoke at a Catholic high school. After the chapel service, one student who had heard me speak came up and said, "Thank you for your message, Father." The student next to him elbowed him in the ribs and said in a stage whisper, "He ain't no real Father. He's got two kids!" Labels are a real problem for us, aren't they? Through labels we create suspicion, misunderstanding, distancing, paranoia. Through labels, we teach fear, discrimination, bigotry, prejudice, and hatred. In *Living, Loving, and Learning,* Leo Buscaglia expresses it like this:

> Words are supposed to free us. Words are supposed to make us able to communicate. But [too often] words become boxes and bags in which we become trapped. . . . And you don't even know what it means. And so it is, with "Black man," with "Chicano," with "Protestants," with "Catholics," with "Jews." All you have to do is hear a label and you think you know everything about them. No one ever bothers to say, "Does he cry? Does he feel? Does he understand? Does he have hopes? Does he love his kids?" . . .
> *Labels.* The loving individual frees himself from labels. He says, "No more." (pp. 21, 22, 25)

Jesus looked at Zacchaeus that day and refused to be blinded by prejudice. He refused to label him. He saw not a "tax collector," with all the ugly baggage that label carried back then, but a person of worth, a human being, a brother, a child of God—and he called him by name. How beautiful to our ears is the sound of our name!

You know, there are more than 250 different kinds of "Who's Who" lists in America. Recently, as a joke, some college students established a "Who's Nobody" list. A woman from one of our Midwestern states applied. Her name was Helen. Helen said she qualified for the "Who's Nobody" list because she had been seeing the same psychiatrist for three years to work on her self-esteem. Helen said that even though she had been meeting weekly with the psychiatrist for more than three years, he still calls her "Jennifer"!

Jesus didn't make that mistake. He called Zacchaeus

by name—the right name. He entered his life personally, and Zacchaeus was changed personally! He comes to each one of us like that—uniquely, genuinely, personally—and if you will listen closely, you can hear him. You can hear him calling your name, and you can say with the hymn writer, "What a Friend We Have in Jesus"—a friend who can help us and change us and redeem us, a friend who can make us over personally.

Zacchaeus Was Changed Socially

Zacchaeus not only got a new view of himself personally, he also got a new view of other people. He came down out of that sycamore tree, reaching out to others in love.

In the weeks before Easter, our church often has a program I like very much. It's called the Forty Days of Love. It's a six-week sacred opportunity to express love and let people close to us know how much we appreciate and value them. It's a great experience for those who take it seriously and really commit to it.

• The first week is the Week of Letter Writing, when we are urged to write letters to those we appreciate. It might be a letter of love or thanks or encouragement or apology or reconciliation or sympathy.
• The second week is the Week of Phone Calls.
• The third week is the Week of Love Gifts.
• The fourth week is the Week of Prayer.
• The fifth week is the Week of Visits.
• And then we conclude with Holy Week.

Some years ago in another church, I introduced this program one Sunday morning. After church, a good friend came down to talk to me about it. My friend is kind of macho, a former football player who loves to hunt and fish, a strong, self-made man.

He said, "Jim, I love you and I love this church, but I'm not going to participate in this Forty Days of Love stuff. It's O.K. for some folks, but it's a little too sentimental and syrupy for me."

However, the next Sunday, he waited for me after church and said, "I want to apologize for what I said last Sunday about the Forty Days of Love. I realized on Wednesday that I was wrong."

"Wednesday?" I said. "What happened on Wednesday?"

He said, "I got one of those letters! It came as a total surprise, from someone I never expected to hear from like that, and it touched me so deeply that I still have it in my pocket. I have carried that letter ever since I received it. Every time I read it, I get tears in my eyes. I was so moved by that letter, I sat down and wrote ten letters myself."

What a change! That kind of change happened to Zacchaeus that day in Jericho, and it can happen to you and me! Christ can come into our lives and make us the instruments of his love and peace. He can change us personally—and socially.

Zacchaeus Was Changed Spiritually

Zacchaeus got a new view of himself personally. He got a new view of others socially and spiritually. He got a new view of God. Christ came and showed him that God is not to be evaded or avoided or appeased, but rather to be welcomed into our lives, into our homes, into our world, as a trusted friend.

Michelangelo, the master painter and sculptor, once

bought a rock of low-grade marble. As he lugged it home, his neighbor and fellow artist laughed at him and chided him: "What is this ugly cheap rock you've purchased? You'll be wasting your time on that."

Michelangelo replied simply: "There is an angel trapped in this stone, and I must set it free!" He worked patiently and carefully, and gradually, under his masterful chisel, the stone's imperfections were transformed into a beautiful angel!

Isn't this what happens to us when the Master Sculptor gets hold of our lives? That which is ugly and low grade is chipped away, and we become a new creation by the touch of the Master's hand. God has lots of life-changing moments for us. If only we would wake up and see them, and seize them, and celebrate them! Personally, socially, spiritually, he's making us over. We can't just be the same anymore!

6.

When You Have Spiritual Cataracts

Matthew 6:22-23: The eye is the lamp of the body. So, if your eye is healthy, your whole body will be full of light; but if your eye is unhealthy, your whole body will be full of darkness. If then the light in you is darkness, how great is the darkness!

Recently I asked a friend in the medical profession to give me a good definition of a cataract. The description given to me was even better and more helpful than I had expected it to be. As you read it, think with me about what might be spiritual cataracts for us:

In medical terms, a cataract is a clouding over of the lens of the eye. This "filminess" causes a loss of transparency and obstructs the passage of light into the eye, thereby causing "distorted vision." There is no pain: The loss of vision is gradual; it slips up on you. The cataract abnormality may occur in younger people as a result of some trauma, but most commonly it occurs in adults. If left unattended, the cloudiness may become so heavy that no light can get through at all and vision is lost altogether. Cataracts can be removed by surgery.

This medical description brings to mind the words of Jesus in Matthew 6: "The eye is the lamp of the body. If your eye is sound, your whole body will be full of light; but if your eye is not sound, your whole body will be full of darkness."

It is interesting to note here that in the Greek language, the original language of the New Testament, the word for *body* often meant more than the physical anatomy. It often meant what we in the twentieth century would call the total personality.

With that in mind, let me paraphrase Jesus: "The eye is the lamp of the total personality." In other words, the way we see things, the way we look at things, the way we view things, the perspective we bring to things, says a lot about us and our spiritual lives. The way we view our job, material things, the world, life, says a lot about our spiritual health.

You may remember that episode in the old Andy Griffith show when Barney Fife, the nervous deputy of Mayberry, decides to become an amateur psychiatrist. He sends off for an amateur psychiatric kit. When it arrives, he tries it out on Otis, the town drunk, using the classic ink-blot test.

Barney shows Otis one of the ink blots and says, "Look at this, Otis, and tell me what you see!"

Otis answers, "I see a bat!"

Barney gets upset and says, "That's the difference between you and me, Otis! You see a bat and I see a butterfly!"

Well, for once in his life, Barney was precisely on target—the difference between people is indeed often most clearly demonstrated by the way we see things. Someone put it like this:

> Two men looked out through prison bars.
> One saw mud; the other saw stars.

When Jesus implies that we should beware of "spiritual cataracts," he is reminding us that there are certain obvious things that can blind our eyes, that can cloud and distort our vision.

What might those things be? That is the question before us now. What are some spiritual cataracts that can "fuzzy up" our vision? What comes to your mind? Let me share a few I can think of. I'm sure you will think of others.

Prejudice Is a Spiritual Cataract

I don't know of anything that can distort our vision more than prejudice. It blinds us!

Some years ago when I left Tennessee to go to seminary, I went to the Methodist Theological School in Ohio. I was a little nervous about going "up north" for the first time. My first day on campus, I was introduced to a student from Michigan. When he heard that I was a southerner from Tennessee, he immediately became very hostile.

"A southerner, huh!" he said with anger. "I know about you people! You should be ashamed of yourself! I know how you treat minority groups! I know about your prejudice!" Well, that hurt! And it made me mad, too.

But I was able somehow to maintain my composure, and I said quietly, "Do you know what the word *prejudice* means?"

"Of course I do," he retorted. "It means to prejudge, to write people off, to judge them negatively without really knowing them."

"That's right," I answered, "and I think that's what you just did to me."

There was a moment of silence. He looked at me fiercely, and I thought for an instant that maybe I had gone too far.

But then his face softened and he replied, "I believe you are right, and I think I owe you an apology. I'm sorry." He put his hand out and I shook it. From that moment we became close friends, and still are.

Prejudice is a terrible thing. To lump people into groups is blind and unfair and often very cruel. To think all musicians are alike, to think all women are alike, to think all southerners or northerners are alike, is wrong. To lump all artists, or all young people, or all people over age thirty into a group is unfair. To think that all teachers, or all psychiatrists, or all African Americans, or all Hispanics, or all red-haired people are the same, is blind and wrong.

At best, it is narrow stereotyping. At worst, it is heart-breaking cruelty! Prejudice distorts the vision because it will not look at new facts. It is lazy and it is unchristian. It blinds us to the uniqueness and individuality of each of God's children. Prejudice is a spiritual cataract that clouds our vision of other people.

Narrowness Is a Spiritual Cataract

Narrowness, tunnel vision, closed-mindedness—whatever you want to call it—is a spiritual cataract. Interestingly, my friend in the medical profession told me that one of the consequences of a cataract as it begins to grow on your eye is that you lose your peripheral vision. You can see in only one direction! That's what closed-mindedness is—the inability to see anybody else's way.

There is an old story about a major league baseball

manager who needed some help for his team when they were in the thick of a heated pennant race. He sent his best scout down to the minors to find a good hitter. The next day the scout called back so excited he could hardly speak.

"I've found just the player we need," he said. "He's terrific! With this guy, we can win the World Series! It's unbelievable how good he is! He could come to the major leagues today and become an instant star! He is, without question, the best baseball player I have ever seen!"

The manager asked, "Can he hit?"

"Well, no," admitted the scout. "He's a pitcher, but he pitched a perfect game. Every throw was in the strike zone. He didn't walk anybody. He struck out every batter—a no-hitter, a perfect game! In fact, only one player on the other team touched the ball with the bat, and that was a foul tip!"

The manager said, "Forget about the pitcher! Sign the guy who fouled one off. What we need is a hitter!"

Well, the point is clear. The narrow view blinds us to new possibilities. The manager's mind was made up that the only way to help his team was with a new hitter, and blinded by the narrow view, he missed the greatest player of all time! Narrowness is a spiritual cataract because it blinds us to new opportunities, new possibilities, new truths, and new ways.

Jealousy Is a Spiritual Cataract

Have you ever heard the expression "He's so jealous he can't see straight"? That's pretty much on target. It fits. Resentment of others clouds our view. Envy distorts our vision. Jealousy does indeed blind us!

Shakespeare knew about this. He wrote one of his most famous plays about it. Remember Othello? Othello loved Desdemona, and she loved him. But then Iago planted the seed of doubt in Othello's mind—the seed of jealousy! In the end, Othello smothered his beloved and innocent Desdemona to death with a pillow, because his jealousy had driven him into a blind rage. That is what jealousy does to us. And Shakespeare was right in calling it a tragedy, because it is tragic when prejudice or narrowness or jealousy become spiritual cataracts.

There are many other spiritual cataracts we could mention—fear, despair, hate, selfishness—these too can distort our vision. But remember the text: "If your eye is healthy, your whole body will be full of light; but if your eye is unhealthy, your whole body will be full of darkness." William Barclay translates this in a helpful way: "If the eye is generous, there is light. If the eye is grudging, there is darkness."

If we want to have 20-20 vision spiritually, then the way to do it is to let the Great Physician come into our lives and perform surgery to take away everything in us that is grudging. Then we can see everything and everybody with the eye of generosity, the eye of goodwill, the eye of compassion, the eye of love. Hymn writer Clara H. Scott said it beautifully:

> Open my eyes, that I may see
>   glimpses of truth thou hast for me;
> place in my hands the wonderful key
>   that shall unclasp and set me free.
>
> Silently now I wait for thee,
>   ready, my God, thy will to see.
> Open my eyes, illumine me,
> Spirit divine!

7.

When You Must Face a Giant

I Samuel 17:37-40: David said, "The Lord, who saved me from the paw of the lion and from the paw of the bear, will save me from the hand of this Philistine." So Saul said to David, "Go, and may the Lord be with you!"

Saul clothed David with his armor; he put a bronze helmet on his head and clothed him with a coat of mail. David strapped Saul's sword over the armor, and he tried in vain to walk, for he was not used to them. Then David said to Saul, "I cannot walk with these; for I am not used to them." So David removed them. Then he took his staff in his hand, and chose five smooth stones from the wadi, and put them in his shepherd's bag, in the pouch; his sling was in his hand, and he drew near to the Philistine.

It's still happening. Old men start wars; young men and women have to fight them. We see a classic example of this as far back as early Old Testament times. Way back in I Samuel 17, we find the famous and popular story of David and Goliath. There we read about how the small shepherd boy, David, armed only with his trusty slingshot, was sent out to do battle against the most powerful warrior in the Philistine army, a giant of a man named Goliath. Even his name sounds fearsome, doesn't it? Goliath! You wouldn't want to meet him in a dark alley at night.

This famous story celebrates the universal emotion to pull for the underdog. It also marks the beginning of David's meteoric rise to prominence as one of Israel's greatest leaders and heroes.

The Philistines were quite a threat in those days. They were the swaggering military bullies of that time, and they enjoyed kicking sand in the faces of their enemies. They did it with gusto! Because of their monopoly on iron, the Philistines had an edge on everybody. They had superior weapons, extraordinary armor, and better mobility because they could build and use chariots. In addition, they had well-trained, well-disciplined soldiers, who strutted about with bold confidence.

On the other hand, the Israelites were so ill-equipped and so poorly prepared that at first glance any military expert would look at this situation and say, "It's hopeless for the Israelites. They are done for. The party's over. They don't have a chance against the mighty Philistine army." And on top of all that, the Philistines had a not-so-secret weapon—a powerful giant warrior who struck panic into the heart of almost everyone who saw him, a giant soldier who had the Israelites trembling with fear and quaking in their boots.

Goliath, the giant, was so huge that he towered over everybody and so powerful that he carried a spear most men would not be strong enough to throw. And he was covered from head to toe with the finest protective armor available in that day. He looked and sounded invincible as he screamed out his insulting taunts to the smaller, less properly attired Israelites. Goliath was arrogant and ruthless and mean, and the Israelite soldiers were scared to death of him. No one wanted to face the giant Goliath.

But then along came little David, the shepherd boy. David had come to the front lines to bring food and supplies for his older brothers, who were soldiers in the Israelite army. That's the way it worked back then. Since there was no strong central government, there were no K-rations, no C-rations, no MREs (meals ready to eat), no supplies at all. Each soldier had to be fed and equipped by his own family.

Therefore, father Jesse had sent his young son David to the battlefront to bring provisions. Evidently David was too young to join the army and had to stay home with his family, tending the sheep. However, when David arrived at the front and heard the brash, haughty taunts of Goliath, he immediately volunteered to battle the giant.

King Saul hesitated to send this inexperienced young boy out to challenge the mighty giant, but finally the king gave in and consented when he realized David's resolute determination: "David said, 'The LORD, who saved me from the paw of the lion and from the paw of the bear, will save me from the hand of this Philistine.' "

Trying to be helpful, King Saul called for his best armor and put it on David. But that didn't work at all. It was too big, too heavy, too cumbersome, and David could barely move in it. So David said, "Thanks, but no thanks. I can't wear another man's armor. I have to do it my way." He took off the heavy armor and set it aside. And then he went out to face the giant, armed only with a slingshot, five smooth stones, and the absolute confidence that God would go with him and see him through. Armed with that blessed assurance, David was not afraid. Rather, he was poised, courageous, and confident.

Now, when Goliath saw little David, of all people, coming out to face him, the giant warrior was both amused and insulted—amused that so unlikely a foe had the nerve to confront him, and insulted that they would stoop to sending out a small, inexperienced shepherd boy—with no armor, no sword, no spear—to do battle with him, the most feared warrior of that time. The more Goliath thought about it, the more livid he became, and he felt no sympathy at all for his young opponent. Brashly, the giant moved forward to make quick work of young David.

But David had a surprise for Goliath. With his dependable slingshot, young David struck the giant at his only vulnerable place—right between the eyes, on his forehead—and the giant went down to defeat. When the Philistines saw their champion cut down by a little shepherd boy, they promptly went into a panic and ran away full of fear.

Now, what can we learn from this colorful ancient story? How does it impact our lives today? What does it have to say to you and me right now? What are the timeless lessons here for the living of these days? Well, actually, there are many wonderful insights for us here.

• For one thing, we see the importance of facing our fears squarely—not running away from them, but facing them head-on.
• And we see the amazing strength and courage that come from a sense of God's presence with us.
• And we also see the power of a purpose, the incredible energy that comes from standing tall for what is right and good—the vigor and vitality that come from a great commitment, especially when that commitment is to God.

In one of his Indian stories, Rudyard Kipling wrote these humorous words: "There is only one thing more terrible in battle than a regiment of desperadoes . . . and that is a company of Scotch Presbyterians who rise from their knees and go into action convinced that they are about to do the will of God" (*Interpreter's Bible*, I Sam., p. 979).

Now, of course, all these insights are supremely important, but I want us to zero in on another significant truth that is especially crucial for us today: At one time or another, every single one of us will face a giant! The story of David and Goliath may seem long ago and far away, but this truth is as near as breathing. At some point in your life, you will have to do battle with a fearsome giant.

Your Goliath may come to you in the middle of the night. It may come when you least expect it. It may come suddenly and with no warning. But one thing you can be sure of, one thing you can count on—it will come! The giant you face may come in a hospital room. You may meet it in a doctor's clinic or a lawyer's office. It may come in a phone call from one of your children. It may come at work—or it may come from the lips of your spouse.

Your Goliath may be called *cancer* or *heart failure* or *alcohol*. It may be called *divorce* or *grief* or *disappointment* or *rejection* or *betrayal* or *temptation* or *sin* or *tragedy*. It may take the shape of loss of mate, loss of job, loss of health, loss of face, or loss of security. But one way or another, one thing is sure—each of us, at some time or another, will face that fearsome giant; we will have to do battle with our own personal Goliath.

Now, with that in mind, let me ask you this: What can we learn from David that will equip us, prepare us for that hard moment when we face our giant? Let me underscore three helpful thoughts that emerge from this Scripture in I Samuel 17.

First, Be Yourself

When you have to face your giant, be yourself! Notice in verse 39 that David couldn't wear Saul's armor. You know why, don't you? Because he wasn't Saul! He was David! Saul's armor wouldn't work for him. It didn't fit. When he put it on, it felt cumbersome, and he looked ludicrous in it. David had to be himself! He had to do it *his* way! So this is the first lesson—be yourself!

Dr. Ellsworth Kalas was the speaker at a recent workshop on preaching. He used to teach the art of preaching, and he said his biggest problem was to persuade the young preachers to create their own style. He would say to the students, "Don't be a copy cat! Don't be a counterfeit!" The students, he said, were always tempted to try to copy some favorite teacher or preacher, or to change their manner of speaking when they went into the pulpit. They would try to speak in a pious, holy-sounding tone, and they would sound so unreal, so fake, so counterfeit. It's good counsel for preachers, and indeed for everybody, so don't be a copy cat, and don't be counterfeit. Be yourself!

My brother, Bob Moore, who also is a minister, likes to tell a story about a great boxer of another generation, Billy Conn. In 1941, Billy Conn almost became the heavyweight champion of the world. Through thirteen rounds, he followed his plan and strategy, using his quickness and speed to build up points. It worked to perfection. He was way ahead on points, beating Joe Louis, the champion.

Billy Conn only needed to continue this for two more rounds, and he would become the heavyweight champion of the world! But suddenly he abandoned his plan and decided to slug it out with Joe Louis. He wanted to win with a knock-out. You know what happened, don't you? Joe Louis knocked him out! Billy Conn tried to wear someone else's armor. He tried to fight the way somebody else fought. He tried to be something he was not, and because of that he was an "almost" champion.

I saw this on a bumper sticker recently: "God made you, and he knew what he was doing!" That's just another way of saying, "Celebrate you! Be authentic. Be genuine. Don't go into battle wearing someone else's armor!" In other words, "Be yourself!"

Second, Draw Strength from God

When you must face a giant, draw strength from God. See how this is expressed in verse 45: "But David said to the Philistine, 'You come to me with sword and spear and javelin; but I come to you in the name of the LORD'" (I Sam. 17:45). David drew his courage, his strength, and his confidence from the bold certainty that God was with him.

One of the greatest comedy acts in the history of show business was the beloved husband and wife team of George Burns and Gracie Allen. In real life, Gracie Allen was a bright, wise businesswoman, but she always played the part of a naive, off-the-wall personality, sweetly simple in her approach to life.

On one of their radio programs, Gracie became very upset because her new electric clock kept losing time. Each day it lost lots of time, so she finally called a repairman. He discovered the answer immediately. There was nothing wrong with the clock. The only problem was that the electric clock was not plugged in!

Gracie Allen said, "I know that! I didn't want to waste electricity, so I only plug it in when I want to know what time it is!"

That's the way some people treat their faith, isn't it? They are not plugged in to the power source! They only plug in when they want something! Not so with David. He stayed plugged in to God. He knew that God would be with him this time because God had been with him before. God had helped him before, delivered him before, saved him before. God was his ever-ready power source.

This is the good news of the Bible. God is the power source, and God is always with us. We can draw incredible strength from God when we stay plugged in. When you must face a giant, be yourself, and then draw strength from God.

And Third, Trust God to See You Through

Her name was Ann. She was thirty-two, and she was battling the biggest, most fearsome giant she had ever confronted. Her Goliath was a brain tumor. She had undergone extensive surgery and was facing months and months of painstaking therapy.

"How's it going?" I said to her one morning at the hospital.

"It's been tough," she answered, "real tough, but I'm hopeful. I'm optimistic. I don't know exactly how this will all turn out, but one thing I do know is that God is with me—and God will see me through!"

Like David, Ann did her best and trusted God to bring it out right. We can do that, too, when we face our giant. Like David, we can be ourselves, we can draw strength from God, and we can trust God to see us through.

8.

When You Feel Inadequate

John 6:~~1-13~~: One of his disciples, Andrew, Simon Peter's brother, said to him, "There is a boy here who has five barley loaves and two fish. But what are they among so many people?" Jesus said, "Make the people sit down." Now there was a great deal of grass in the place; so they sat down, about five thousand in all. Then Jesus took the loaves and when he had given thanks, he distributed them to those who were seated; so also the fish, as much as they wanted. When they were satisfied, he told his disciples, "Gather up the fragments left over, so that nothing may be lost." So they gathered them up, and from the fragments of the five barley loaves, left by those who had eaten, they filled twelve baskets.

*S*ee if you can find the common thread that runs through these three little stories.

• There is an old legend from India about a huge elephant and a tiny mouse who became very close friends. They walked everywhere together, side by side. One day they came to a long narrow bridge, suspended over a deep gorge. Side by side, they stepped onto the bridge and walked across.

When they stepped off at the other side, the little mouse turned to the elephant and proclaimed proudly, "Wow! We sure made that old bridge shake, didn't we?"

• Without question, Michael Jordan is one of the greatest athletes in the world today. The popular star of the Chicago Bulls professional basketball team is considered by many to be the most outstanding basketball player to ever play the game.

In the play-offs a couple of years ago, when the pressure was greatest and the competition was toughest, Jordan made 63 points in one game. A few days later, one of his teammates was being interviewed on television. This particular player is not a superstar, but he is a solid player who comes off the bench to help his team.

The interviewer said to him, "Even though you have never led the league in scoring or made the All Star team, can you think of any special highlight in your NBA career?"

With tongue positioned firmly in his cheek, the player answered, "Well, I'll never forget the night Michael Jordan and I combined for 65 points!"

• In the sixth chapter of John, we find the story of Jesus' feeding of the five thousand. With five barley loaves and two fish provided by a little boy, he miraculously feeds that vast multitude of people. One legend connected to the story tells that after the miracle, the little boy who had provided the food made his way home and ran into his house, shouting: "Mama! Mama! you'll never guess what Jesus and I did today!"

So, what is the common thread in these stories? Of course, it is the fact that when we join forces with a greater strength, we can indeed do incredible things together. The spiritual message is obvious: God can take our little and make it much! If we will simply offer what we have, humble though it may be, God can use it in amazing and miraculous ways.

That's what this marvelous story in John 6 is all about. The boy in the story brought his little, and God made it enough, and then some. The five barley loaves and two fish were probably the contents of the little boy's picnic lunch. Barley bread, by the way, was the food of the very poor in Bible times. It was the cheapest, the kind most people back then fed to their animals.

The two fish, in all likelihood, were small pickled fish, something to help moisten the dry barley bread. In those days, with no refrigeration, fresh fish would have been quite a luxury, not something a small boy from a poor family would have in his lunch basket. But nevertheless, meager as it was, the little boy brought what he had to Jesus, and our Lord used it. My, how he used it!

William Barclay, in *The Gospel of John,* put it like this: "There was the boy. He had not much to offer but out of what he had, Jesus found the materials of a miracle. There would have been one great and shining deed fewer in history if that boy had . . . withheld his loaves and fishes." The point is that Jesus can use what we bring him. It may not be much, but he can use it. Barclay goes on:

> It may well be that the world is denied miracle after miracle and triumph after triumph because we will not bring to Christ what we have and what we are. If, just as we are, we would lay ourselves on the altar of the service of Jesus Christ, there is no saying what Christ could do with us and through us. We may be sorry and embarrassed that we have not more to bring—and rightly so; but that is no reason for failing or refusing to bring what we have and what we are. Little is always much in the hands of Christ. (Vol. 1, pp. 207-208)

This feeding-of-the-five-thousand episode must have made a deep impression on the disciples, because it is the only miracle, other than the resurrection, in the whole ministry of Jesus that is recorded in all four Gospels. The story was familiar to me when I looked at it again recently, but I saw something new and fresh this time. I was amazed to discover just how relevant it is to the particular issue of coping with life's difficulties.

This story depicts Jesus and his disciples up against a real down-to-earth problem, and the way he responded is both fascinating and enlightening. Jesus and his disciples had retreated to the more private eastern shore of the Sea of Galilee to reflect and pray, but the people had followed them. One of the great things about Jesus was that he never looked on needy human beings as a nuisance. Instead, out of deep compassion, he rearranged his plans and worked with these interruptions creatively and meaningfully.

Now, his disciples were more like we are. They weren't nearly so patient or gracious. "Oh no! Here they come again! Why can't they just leave us alone!" The disciples were worn to a frazzle by the crowd and wanted to get rid of them. They also realized that the people were hungry and tired, and they knew full well that crowds in that condition could become hostile and get out of hand.

So they began to strategize. They took Jesus to one side and pointed out the difficulty, suggesting that he disperse the people quickly before things went from bad to worse. It was a perfectly natural suggestion, in the face of the situation Jesus and the disciples were facing—a situation full of stress and potential danger.

But look closely at the way Jesus coped with the problem. And notice that his response is a beautiful model for us in coping with problems—and a powerful reminder that God can take our little and make it much.

As we study this powerful story, three important lessons emerge. Interestingly, the three key lessons are wrapped up in the attitudes of the three main characters in the story.

There Is the Attitude of Jesus:
He Chose to Cope Rather Than Run

Jesus chose to face the crowd. He refused to follow the disciples' suggestion that they employ the strategy of escape. He decided instead to face the situation squarely and openly, with confidence and optimism. He saw the problem as an opportunity.

Instead of saying, "Trouble is coming; let's go our way and let them go theirs," he said, "We are involved in this event together. We cannot pass the buck. Let's face it and deal with it, creatively and productively." Then, with the help of the Father, he fed the people.

It is clear from this response that, for Jesus, the way *out* was always the way *through*. To him, the solution to the problem could not be found by running or hiding, but by facing it squarely and courageously, facing it with trust in the Father.

Eileen Egan has worked with Mother Teresa for more than thirty years. In *Such a Vision of the Street*, she describes Mother Teresa's amazing approach to life. She tells about the day she was talking to Mother Teresa about all the problems that faced them, rattling off a depressing list of difficulties.

Then Mother Teresa, with a warm smile, said, "Do we have to call everything a problem? Why not erase the word *problem* from our vocabulary and instead use the word *gift?*"

Eileen Egan said, "From that time on, items that presented disappointments or difficulties would be introduced with 'We have a small gift here' or 'Today we have an especially big gift.' "

75

Now there were smiles when confronted with situations that earlier had been described by the dour word *problem.* In a wonderful way, Mother Teresa has captured the spirit of our Lord, the spirit of seeing problems as opportunities. That's the first lesson we learn here. We see it in the attitude of Jesus as he chose to cope, rather than run.

There Is the Attitude of Andrew: He Found the Available Resources and Brought Them Forward

This was the greatness of Andrew: He was always bringing somebody to Jesus. He could find the available resources and bring them to our Lord. Earlier, he had brought his brother, and now he brings this little boy with his picnic lunch. Even though Andrew wonders about the small amount of the resources, he nevertheless brings the boy and his lunch basket to Jesus and lets Jesus take it from there.

Sometimes we fail to do this. A problem may loom so large and seem so formidable that we suffer from tunnel vision, closed-mindedness, and as a result, we are blinded to the available resources, the available tools, the available opportunities. We don't even see them. We throw up our hands, blinded by our emotions, and cry, "What's the use!"

Several singers have recorded the beautiful song, "From a Distance." Have you heard it? It has a beautiful melody with haunting lyrics:

> God is watching us, God is watching us . . .
> From a distance.

What does this song mean? What's the message?

Maybe it means that when we back away from some-thing, we can see it better. When we back away from our emotions, our pride, our selfishness, aggression, preju-dices, and hostilities, things come into better focus.

Maybe it reminds us that God, from his perspective, can see how it ought to be in this world; and with God's vision and help, we could have hope and love and peace.

Maybe it reminds us that God can see the big picture, and in the big picture, God wants all his children to live together in harmony.

And maybe it reminds us that God is watching us, and ultimately, we are accountable to God for the way we handle the resources of this world.

In John 6, Jesus chose to cope with the problem rather than run from it. And Andrew found the available resources and brought them forward.

There Is the Attitude of the Boy: He Trusted Jesus to Take His Little and Make It Much

Of course, the key word is *trust*. That is our calling as Christians—to be faithful to the best we know, and then trust God to see us through.

Some years ago, two scientists were on a field trip in the mountains. They discovered a baby eagle in a nest on a crag, just below the top of a steep and dangerous cliff. The baby eagle had been deserted and they wanted to rescue it. They asked the young son of their guide if they could lower him on a rope to fetch the eaglet.

The boy was not at all enthused by their plan, so he declined. They offered him money, then doubled it, but still the boy refused.

Finally, one of the scientists asked in despair, "Do you

have any suggestions as to how we can save the baby eagle?"

The mountain boy replied, "Sure! I'll go down to rescue the bird for free, if you'll let my dad hold the rope!"

He trusted his dad completely. He knew he could count on his dad. He knew his dad would not let him down. With that kind of trust, the little boy in John 6 handed over his lunch to Jesus—and Jesus did not fail him. He took his little and made it much. That's the good news of our faith. We don't have to be overwhelmed by feelings of inadequacy, because God can, indeed, take our little and make it much! Annie Johnson Flint put it like this:

> God hath not promised
>   Skies always blue,
> Flower-strewn pathways
>   All our lives through;
> God hath not promised
>   Sun without rain,
> Joy without sorrow,
>   Peace without pain.
>
> But God hath promised
>   Strength for the day,
> Rest for the labor,
>   Light for the way,
> Grace for the trials,
>   Help from above,
> Unfailing sympathy,
>   Undying Love.

9.

When You Have Swallowed Spiritual Poison

Mark 7:14 16, 21 23. 1—23 Then he called the crowd again and said to them, "Listen to me, all of you, and understand: there is nothing outside a person that by going in can defile, but the things that come out are what defile. . . . For it is from within, from the human heart, that evil intentions come: fornication, theft, murder, adultery, avarice, wickedness, deceit, licentiousness, envy, slander, pride, folly. All these evil things come from within, and they defile a person."

Not too long ago, I was the speaker for a retreat in east Texas. While there, I accidentally cut my finger. It looked pretty bad to me, so I rushed off to the camp infirmary. There I found a nurse who could easily have volunteered as a Marine drill sergeant. She was working a crossword puzzle. When I walked in, she hardly looked up.

"I cut my finger," I said. "It looks pretty serious."

After a quick, bored glance, she said, "The bandages are in the medicine cabinet over there."

"Bandages," I said. "Don't you think I need more than that—like stitches, a tourniquet, a cold compress, a doctor, a blood transfusion?"

She looked up from her crossword puzzle again just long enough to roll her eyes unsympathetically and, without moving a muscle, she said it again—this time more firmly: "The bandages are in the medicine cabinet over there."

I thought to myself, "Here I am, about to bleed to death, and she's working a crossword puzzle and talking about bandages." I walked over to the sink and washed my finger and looked at it again. And I had to admit it really wasn't so bad after all.

Then when I opened the medicine cabinet to search for a bandage, my eyes fell on a large brown bottle. On it was written in bold letters: WARNING! POISONOUS WHEN TAKEN INTERNALLY! At the bottom of the label, an antidote was given, just in case someone inadvertently swallowed the poison. When I saw those words, my mind flashed back to Dr. D. L. Dykes' description of the one person he ever knew who had taken poison:

> She did it to commit suicide. She was twenty years old. I was a minister at the time in my first pastorate.
>
> I remember, as if it were yesterday, going to the hospital and seeing her lips parched and swollen, turned outward as they burned with the poison, and how she pleaded with her mother and the doctor to save her. But it was too late. The poison had already taken its toll, and a few hours later she died in her mother's arms. It was a horrible thing to see—one of the worst things I have ever seen in my life.

As I thought of that recently, I realized that there is another way we poison ourselves. There is another kind of poison just as dangerous and, ultimately, just as deadly. Spiritual poison—lethal attitudes that eat us up, burn us up, destroy us, poison us when taken internally—attitudes that will devastate us if they take root in our souls. This is precisely what Jesus is talking about in Mark 7—spiritual poisons!

Now, none of us will ever intentionally take poison, but all of us run the risk of being poisoned spiritually. It is an ever-present threat that we constantly have to fight off. We dare not let these spiritual poisons get inside us. They are dangerous when taken internally. Spiritual poisons—there are many of them. Let me list just a few.

Selfishness Is a Spiritual Poison

There is a humorous story about a young woman who wrote a love letter to her former fiance:

Dear Tommy,
    Can you ever forgive me? No words could ever express the great unhappiness I've felt since breaking our engagement. Please say you'll take me back. No one could ever take your place in my heart, so please forgive me. I love you! I love you! I love you!
                                        Yours forever,
                                        Marie
P.S. And congratulations on winning the state lottery!

Selfishness can be humorous in a joke or in a cartoon, but in real life, it is no laughing matter. Selfishness sometimes can even be cute in a little child, but it's always ugly, tragic, and destructive in a grown-up. Jesus and the apostle Paul saw it as a spiritual poison, an enemy of life and love.

Some years ago, James Barrie wrote a little half-hour play titled *The Will.* A happy newlywed couple enter a lawyer's office to draw up a will. The husband has inherited some money, and he wants to complete the will in a single sentence, leaving everything to his wife. She lovingly protests at being the sole beneficiary and insists on a clause by which their little wealth would be shared with his cousins and a convalescent home.

The lawyer, deeply impressed with their refreshing unselfishness, pats them on the back as they leave and says, "You are a ridiculous couple. But please don't change."

Twenty years later, they come back to make a new will, now involving a sizable estate. The wife has come along to make sure the husband does nothing foolish. She wrangles with him when he wants to include his cousins, and the poor convalescent home is dropped completely. Each refers to the estate as "my money," and only after bitter argument is any agreement reached at all.

Twenty more years pass, and the husband, now knighted and sixty-five years old, comes in alone. The wife is dead. The children, he says, have turned out to be "rotters." This time, he has come to cancel all previous wills, cutting off all his relatives without a penny.

He starts to dictate to the lawyer: "I leave it . . . I leave it —oh my God, I don't know what to do with it!" He paces the floor and, at last, shouts angrily, "Here are the names of half a dozen men I fought to get my money. I beat them. So leave it to them, with my curses!"

Selfishness is a spiritual poison. It is so dangerous, so devastating, so deadly. Remember how Jesus put it: "What shall it profit us if we gain the whole world and lose our own souls?"

Greed Is a Second Spiritual Poison

In the cartoon "Sally Forth," Hilary looks at their big Christmas tree with all the presents beneath it and says, "Mom, have you ever noticed how one particular emotion gets real strong at Christmas?"

Her mother answers, "I sure have, honey. I get so very nostalgic at this time of year. I especially like to think back to Christmases when I was your age. My mind fills with warm memories of decorating the tree, singing carols, baking cookies. It's a big part of the holidays for me. And I am so impressed that someone your age would recognize that nostalgia is such a strong emotion at Christmastime."

Hilary goes back to the tree, looks at the huge pile of wrapped gifts, and thinks to herself, "Nostalgia! I was talking about *greed!*"

Dick Milham, one of America's top convention speakers, uses an ancient Lebanese legend to show how poisonous greed can be. According to the legend, two shepherds were caring for their flocks when they heard the screams of a man in desperate trouble. They ran toward the river and saw an older man struggling in the rapid water, being dragged to his death. One shepherd dove into the water, the other threw in a lifeline, and the rescue was made.

As the older man lay on the ground, he made a startling statement: "You have shown great courage and saved my life. Now, I have the power to give you a great gift. Either of you may wish for anything you desire, and you will receive it. And the other of you will receive twice as much!"

At first, the two shepherds thought the man might be crazy, but after he left, they decided that if he did have that power, they should be careful and take it seriously.

One of them turned to the other and said, "You go ahead and wish."

He started to, but then remembered that the other man would get twice as much, so he said, "No, you go ahead and wish first." In the beginning, it was like a game. They kidded each other about the wealth, but as time passed, it became more serious.

One of them would think, "I'd like a mountain of gold, but he would get two mountains of gold."

The other would think, "I'd like an ocean of diamonds, but he would get two oceans of diamonds."

So the tension grew, the anger increased, and the friendship crumbled. Finally one night, one shepherd could take it no longer. He seized the other by the throat and started choking him, screaming, "Wish! Wish now! Or I will kill you!"

And in that moment, the startled man looked into the hate-filled face of his one-time friend and gasped, "I wish . . . I wish . . . to be made blind in my right eye!" So he was made blind in one eye, and the other man, blind in both eyes, stumbled in darkness for the rest of his life! The point is graphically clear—greed destroys! Greed, like selfishness, is a spiritual poison.

Envy Is a Third Spiritual Poison

Envy is deceptive and sneaky. It doesn't sound so bad, but let me tell you, it is lethal. Envy can devastate our souls.

One of the finest plays and motion pictures of recent years is *Amadeus*—an entertaining dramatization of the life of Mozart. The central figure in the drama is Antonio Salieri, a composer who was a contemporary of Mozart. Salieri was a great talent. He wrote beautiful music, became a big success, and was made chief composer in the emperor's court.

But then one day he heard the music of Mozart, and he recognized that Mozart had gifts far superior to his own. Something happened within Salieri. He became obsessed with the desire to destroy Mozart. He railed against God. He thought God was mocking him through Mozart. Though he had great gifts, great talent, he knew he was not as good as Mozart, and he couldn't stand it. It consumed and ruined his life. It's a tragic portrayal of the poisonous power of envy to destroy the heart and soul.

You know, the only really happy people in the world are those who never feel jealousy and envy. The happiest people are those who enjoy the good fortune of others. Selfishness, greed, envy—all are spiritual poisons. And we need the antidote that comes only in Christ, our Lord. The love he brings us, the love he teaches us, the love he puts within us—that is the antidote that cleanses and heals. The only cure for our spiritual poisons is a heart and soul full of love!

10.

When You Are Having Hearing Problems

Mark 4:2-9: He began to teach them many things in parables, and in his teaching he said to them: " Listen! A sower went out to sow. And as he sowed, some seed fell on the path, and the birds came and ate it up. Other seed fell on rocky ground, where it did not have much soil, and it sprang up quickly, since it had no depth of soil. And when the sun rose, it was scorched; and since it had no root, it withered away. Other seed fell among thorns, and the thorns grew up and choked it, and it yielded no grain. Other seed fell into good soil and brought forth grain, growing up and increasing and yielding thirty and sixty and a hundredfold." And he said, "Let anyone with ears to hear listen!"

Recently I ran across an interesting list, a collection of malapropisms, or "word blunders," on signs written in English in non-English-speaking countries. The words on the signs were "out-of-sync" just enough to confuse the message and produce humorous results. For example:

• In a Bucharest hotel lobby, this sign was posted by the elevator: "The lift is being fixed for the next day. During that time, we regret to tell you that you will be unbearable."
• In a Paris hotel: "Please leave your values at the front desk"!

• In a Norwegian lounge: "Ladies are requested not to have babies in the bar"!

• In an Austrian hotel which caters to skiers, guests were reminded not to walk so loudly down the halls in their ski boots late at night: "Please not to perambulate the corridors in the hours of repose in the boots of ascension"!

• And finally, in a Copenhagen airport: "We take your bags and send them in all directions"! (Alan Sparks, *What Do You Think?*)

Now, we can tell from these fascinating signs that sometimes communication is difficult. Often, we don't get the words right, and consequently the message gets muddled. Even if the words are perfectly stated, communication still does not happen unless somebody is listening! The message may be sent out with power and eloquence, but communication happens only when someone receives the word and responds to it. The art of listening is so important! How is it with you right now? Are you a good listener? Are you tuned in?

Jesus knew about the importance of listening. "Those who have ears to hear, let them hear!" he said. One of Jesus' most powerful parables, the parable of the sower, is about listening. It's about hearing God's Word and responding to it properly.

The sower went out to sow his field, and the seed fell on four different kinds of soil. Some fell on the path, and it couldn't grow because the ground was too hard. Some fell on rocky soil, and because the earth was shallow, the plants sprang up quickly, but then died because they had no roots. Other seed fell among thorns, and the plants tried to grow, but the thorns choked the life out of them. And still other seed fell on good soil, and there the seed grew and yielded a great harvest.

These four different soils represent the different ways people hear and respond to the seed of God's Word: Four different responses to the Gospel, four different kinds of listeners. Let's take a look at these and see if we can find ourselves there.

First, There Is the Path Soil

The path soil represents closed-minded persons who will not listen. Talking to them is like talking to a brick wall. When you go to a farm or a park and you see a path, what is that path like? How would you describe the path soil? Well, of course, it's hard, packed down, like concrete. There's no way it could receive the seed; it's too set and closed.

There are people like that, people who are hard, cynical, set in their ways, calloused, self-centered, crusted-over, closed-minded. These people won't listen. They don't want to hear. They hold God at arm's length. They keep God at a safe distance. They will not let God or his Word penetrate their lives. Their hearts are hard, and their minds are shut.

Dr. Walter Capps teaches in the religion department at the University of California in Santa Barbara. He has developed a nationally famous course that regularly enrolls a thousand students. It's a class on the impact of the Vietnam War on American life and culture. Dr. Capps brings in a lot of guest speakers to talk to the class. Usually they are people who experienced the Vietnam War and the decade of the sixties first-hand.

Early on, a veteran came and talked about returning from Vietnam just when the protests against the war were reaching their height. The young soldier's name was John Murphy. He said he hadn't wanted to go to war. He didn't want to be a soldier. He didn't want to leave his wife, but he was drafted and sent. His government told him to go and fight for the cause of freedom.

And so, he said, "I went and I did the best I could. And I was one of the lucky ones. I survived a horrible year in the jungles of Vietnam. I saw many of my friends killed in action, but I got through it with no serious injuries."

Finally, when John Murphy's army stint was over, he flew directly from the Far East to San Francisco. He had no idea what was happening in the States at the time. All he knew was that he was glad to be safely home, glad to set foot on American soil again. In full-dress uniform, John Murphy got off the plane and ran to a phone booth to call his wife and let her know he was on his way to her arms.

However, when he came out of the telephone booth, he was confronted by an angry war protestor who asked him if he had been to Vietnam. When John Murphy said yes, the man began to curse him, screaming at him and calling him dirty names, spewing out hateful profanity and making obscene gestures. John Murphy tried to explain his situation, but then the protestor spit on him, not once but twice.

John, fresh from combat, could not help himself—he exploded. He grabbed the man and wrestled him to the ground. Fortunately, John said, people ran and pulled them apart, the protestor ran away through the crowd.

John Murphy said, "I couldn't understand what was going on. I felt that I had been representing my country, that I had done my duty, that I had laid my life on the line for the cause of freedom. I had risked my life and had been separated from my family and had seen my friends die—to protect, I thought, his rights, and this was the reaction I got. This was the thanks I got."

John Murphy's voice broke a bit as he spoke. Tears misted his eyes as he completed his story. When he sat down, there was total silence in that auditorium. There were a thousand students there, and you could have heard a pin drop. Complete silence!

Then, far in the back, a young student stood up and said, "I may be a little late with this, but welcome home, John Murphy! Welcome home!" Of course, the hall erupted with applause (Gene Tucker, "The Word of God," *Pulpit Digest*, Sept./Oct. 1991).

I don't understand all of what the Vietnam War and the decade of the sixties were about. But, I do know this: Calling another person profane names, refusing to listen, or spitting on someone who differs with you is wrong! These are dramatic symbols of the closed mind. People on the closed-mind path will not listen, and if you come too close or threaten to disturb their set ways, they will hurt you! Now, please don't misunderstand me. I'm not resurrecting the debate between the hawks and the doves. I'm simply saying that closed-minded people on either side don't help. They make matters worse.

In the first century, the closed-minded people were so threatened by Jesus and his new ideas that they tried to silence him.

"He's stirring up the people with these newfangled ideas; we'd better hit him quick with a cross!" they said, and they crucified him. It's still happening. People with closed minds are still trying to silence Jesus. He tells us, "Love," but they will not listen. He offers, "New life," but they will not respond. He cries, "Follow me," but they will not obey. He says, "Learn of me," but they say, "Sunday school is for kids!"

The path people are hard, calloused, crusted-over. They have ears, but they will not listen or respond because they live in the prison of the closed mind.

Second, There Is the Rocky Soil

The rocky soil represents those who are shallow, who have no staying power. They hear, they get excited, they get fired up—but it doesn't last. They fade quickly because there is no depth, no strength, no roots.

The rocky soil was a thin layer of fertile soil on a thick layer of rock. Because the soil was shallow and fertile, the plant would sprout up immediately. But since it had no way to get its roots down deep, because of that thick layer of rock, the plant would soon shrivel and die. It had no endurance, no lasting life, because there was no depth, no strong root system.

Many people respond to God like that. They get momentarily religious. They get emotionally stirred up. They get excited for awhile, but they never put their roots down. They never get deep into it, and eventually their shallow faith fades away.

I'm thinking of a young couple I talked with some months ago. They said they wanted to marry. But strangely, I had the feeling that what they really wanted was to go on a honeymoon. I wondered if they were really ready for that day-to-day, deep, long-haul commitment it takes to make a marriage work.

Many people are like that in their faith experience. They want to have an exciting honeymoon in the faith, but they are not really ready for the deep, strong, tenacious commitment. They are shallow rocky soil. They hear the gospel and they respond, but it doesn't last, because their faith is too shallow.

Third, There Is the Thorny Soil

The thorny soil represents people who have mixed-up priorities. They give all their energy to the thorns, instead of to the seed.

The summer of 1964 was a significant one for our family, because God had just blessed our home with our first child, a little girl. We named her Jodi, and we were so proud of her. When she was about two months old, we decided it was time to take her to show her off to relatives and friends. So I began the mammoth task of loading the car with all the things you have to take along when you go somewhere with a two-month-old baby. I worked and planned and packed. Finally, I had everything strategically located in the car.

Then I sat down behind the steering wheel, feeling hot and tired, anxious to get on the road, and extremely proud of myself for the ingenious way I had miraculously packed all that baby paraphernalia into our little compact car.

When my wife, June, came out the carport door, I started up the engine ready to go.

"Wait just a minute," she said. "Aren't you about to forget something?"

A little offended by that question, I answered, "That's impossible! I have my checklist here and everything is in the car, checked and double-checked. Just look—suitcases, vaporizer, bassinet, play pen, diapers, diaper bag, bottles, pacifier, formula, baby food, infant seat, powder, shampoo, and Brownie Bear."

"Well," she said, "that's all very nice, but don't you think we should take the baby along, too?"

Sure enough, I had thought of everything but the main thing. The baby was in her room, sound asleep!

I have thought about that incident many times since,

because I see in it a powerful parable for life. Sometimes we get so involved in the "busyness" of life—the details, the mechanics, the trappings, and the checklists—that we forget the most important things.

The point is clear—sometimes we really get our priorities out of whack. Lots of people have that problem when it comes to faith. They give God the back seat, the leftovers! They give all their time and energy to the wrong things, the thorns of life, rather than to the seed of God's Word. They come to church, if and when it's convenient. They sing in the choir, if and when it's convenient. They teach Sunday school or work with the youth, if and when it's convenient. They give their attention and strength to so many other things that God and the church get last place or are left out altogether.

The thorny-soil people have their priorities so mixed up that they are unable to put God first. They have ears, but they hear all the wrong things; they support the thorns, rather than the seed.

Fourth, There Is the Good Soil

The good soil represents those special people who receive God's Word into their lives and work with it to bring forth new life everywhere.

One day I was driving to a speaking engagement in east Texas and listening to a Houston Astros game on the radio. At first the broadcast was coming in loud and clear, but then there was static, and later it faded out altogether. Why? Because I had driven too far from the station! Good-soil hearers are those who stay close to the station!

This sower parable is a tricky one, because when we look at it, as we have in this chapter, we are tempted to categorize people. We might think, well, Joe is a path person; he's so closed-minded. And Betty, she's rocky soil; she gets excited but it never lasts. And Tim, he's thorny soil; he always has his priorities mixed up. And of course, I'm good soil!

That's what we are tempted to do, but that misses the point. For you see, the point is that within you and me, at any given moment, reside all four of these potential soils. At any given moment, we can be path soil, or rocky soil, or thorny soil, or fertile soil. We can be closed-minded, or shallow, or get our priorities mixed up, or we can be good soil and receive God's Word into our lives and work with it to bring forth new life. So the message is clear:

- Be good soil!
- Be good listeners!
- Receive God's Word!
- Love God with your minds!
- Stay close to the station, and stay tuned in!

11

When You Feel Afraid, Confused, Overwhelmed

Acts 2:1- When the day of Pentecost had come, they were all together in one place. And suddenly from heaven there came a sound like the rush of a violent wind, and it filled the entire house where they were sitting. Divided tongues, as of fire, appeared among them, and a tongue rested on each of them. All of them were filled with the Holy Spirit and began to speak in other languages, as the Spirit gave them ability.

In a little book, *Children's Letters to God*, seven-, eight-, and nine-year-old children expressed their faith, their hopes, and their questions. Those letters are wonderful—poignant, humorous, inspiring. The authors, Stuart Hample and Eric Marshall, have written another collection of *Children's Letters to God*. Let me share some of these with you:

• Dear God, In Sunday school, they told us what all you do. Who does it when you are on vacation? (signed) Jane.
• Dear God, I read the Bible. What does *begat* mean? Nobody will tell me. Love, Allison.
• Dear God, I bet it's very hard for you to love everybody in the whole world. There are only four people in our family, and I never can do it. (signed) Nan.
• Dear God, Is it true that my father won't get to go to Heaven if he uses his bowling words in the house? (signed) Anita.

• Dear God, Did you mean for giraffes to look like that, or was it an accident? (signed) Norma.

• Dear God, I went to this wedding and they kissed right in church. Is that O.K.? (signed) Darla.

• Dear God, I wish there wasn't no such thing as sin. I wish there wasn't no such thing as war. (signed) Tim.

• Dear God, I like the Lord's Prayer best of all. Did you have to write it a lot, or did you get it right the first time? I have to write everything I ever write over and over again. Love, Lois.

• Dear God, I think about you sometimes even when I'm not praying. (signed) Elliott.

• Dear God, I don't ever feel alone anymore since I found out about you. Love, Nora.

Out of the mouths of little children come fervent wishes, confessions, confidences, concerns, praise, and thanks. As we read or hear these, we can understand more clearly why Jesus said, "Unless you become like little children, you shall not enter the kingdom of heaven." In a sense, this is what the day of Pentecost is all about. The disciples had to become like little children before they could receive the Holy Spirit. Only then could they take up the torch of Christ's ministry, because only then did they have power from on high.

Go back a few months before that first Pentecost. Remember how the disciples were back then—arrogant, selfish, jealous, haughty, uppity, conceited. Jesus had set his face toward Jerusalem. He was thinking deep thoughts as they walked down that dusty road—thoughts about love and sacrifice and commitment—as he moved steadfastly toward the showdown awaiting him in the Holy City. This was serious business now. He was heading toward the cross!

And what were the disciples doing? They were

walking along behind him, feuding, fussing, and fighting among themselves. Do you remember what they were squabbling about? About which one was the greatest, which ones should get the best seats and the top spots and the most power in the new kingdom. How presumptuous! Jesus was thinking about love and sacrifice and commitment, and all the while, they were quarreling about politics and clout and position.

They were missing the whole point, and Jesus had to go to the cross to get their attention! He had to come out of the tomb to give them their wake-up call! Then they were all ears!

And he said to them, "Here! I want *you* to take up this torch. I want you to take up this ministry of love. I want you to do it now. I want you to be the church. I want you to teach the world this message of love and sacrifice and commitment. Now, I must leave and go to the Father, and you will be my witnesses to all the world."

"But, Lord," they protested, in humility now, "We can't do that! We don't have the strength! We don't have the know-how! We don't have the courage!"

"Don't worry," the Master assured them. "I will send you a helper. I will send you strength and power. I will send the Holy Spirit to be with you always." And with that, Jesus ascended into heaven.

Like little children, the disciples then went back to the security of the upper room—to think this all through, to sort this all out, and to wait for the Holy Spirit. Now, think about this. Their Lord has gone. The task is squarely on their shoulders. They feel so inadequate and so scared, and now they have to sit and wait for this Holy Spirit to come. And they were not very good at waiting! On earlier occasions when Jesus told them to wait, they either, in their impatience, did the wrong thing, or in their apathy, fell asleep.

Now here they are waiting, and I can imagine the conversation in the upper room going something like this:

• Simon Peter, impatient and pacing nervously: "This waiting is driving me up the wall. How long do we have to wait around here anyway? Why can't we get on with this or just forget the whole thing?"

• And doubting Thomas: "We don't know anything about this Holy Spirit. I've never seen any Holy Spirit. I mean, how do we know it really exists? I know we can trust our Lord, but maybe we misunderstood him. Maybe no Holy Spirit is coming after all."

• Next Andrew speaks: "I've always been a good helper, but I don't know how to be a good leader. I'm not sure I can. I'm not wired up that way. I could serve the Lord enthusiastically when he told me what to do, but now he's gone, and I don't know how to do this. I don't know what we are supposed to do."

• Then John: "Look! He told us to wait here. He told us he would send help. I think we can count on that, but I have to tell you honestly, I feel alone without him, and I do feel helpless and inadequate."

• James speaks up: "We've been waiting here a pretty good while and nothing has happened. Maybe Thomas is right. Maybe it's over. Maybe we should just face that and accept that, and give up and go back to our former jobs."

• Simon Peter speaks again: "No! We wait! He told us the Holy Spirit will come, and I believe him. With all my heart, I believe him!"

Just as Simon Peter spoke those words, they heard something—a strange sound way off in the distance,

becoming louder and louder as it moved toward them—
a sound like the rush of a mighty wind. And it blew on
that place—Oh my, did it blow on that place! And they
were all filled with the Holy Spirit. They received
courage and confidence and strength and new life. And
through the power and presence of the Holy Spirit, they
were made whole, and they became the church of the
living God on that Pentecost day. Through the gift of the
Holy Spirit, they were empowered to take up the
preaching, teaching, healing, caring ministry of Jesus
Christ.

In *Who's Coming to Dinner?* Robert Morgan tells a
powerful story about a Dutch pastor and his family, who
got into big trouble with the Nazis during the Second
World War. They had been hiding Jewish people in their
home to keep them safe from Hitler's forces. They were
eventually found out, and one night in the darkness,
they heard the sound of heavy boots and loud, impatient knocking on the door.

They were seized and loaded into a cattle car to be
taken to one of the notorious death camps. All night
long, the pastor and his family rode in heartbreaking
anguish, jostling against one another and the other pris-
oners who were jammed into the car. They were
stripped of any form of dignity and absolutely terrified.
They knew they were being taken to one of Hitler's
extermination centers. But which one? Would it be
Auschwitz, Buchenwald, or Dachau?

Finally, the long night ended and the train stopped.
The doors of the cattle car were opened and light
streamed into that tragic scene. They were marched out
and lined up beside the railroad tracks, resigned to
unspeakable pain, as they knew they would be separated from one another and ultimately killed. But in the
midst of their gloom, they discovered some amazing

good news—good news beyond belief! They discovered, in the bright morning sunlight, that they were not in a death camp at all, not in Germany at all, but in Switzerland! During the night, someone, through personal courage and daring, had tripped a switch and sent the train to Switzerland—and freedom. And those now who came to them were not their captors at all, but their liberators. Instead of being marched to death, they were welcomed to new life.

In the midst of his joy and relief, the Dutch pastor said, "What do you do with such a gift?"

Something like that happened to the disciples at Pentecost. They were afraid, confused, unsure, overwhelmed, and then came this incredible gift—the gift of the Holy Spirit! It turned their lives around, and empowered by this amazing gift, they went out and turned the world upside down!

One of my favorite hymns I first learned as a camp song. It's called *Spirit of the Living God, Fall Afresh on Me*, and it contains these poignant prayer words:

> Melt me, mold me, fill me, use me.
> Spirit of the living God, fall afresh on me.

It's a great song, because it shows us precisely what the Holy Spirit does for us when we are afraid, confused, or overwhelmed. It melts us, molds us, fills us, and uses us. Let me show you what I mean.

The Holy Spirit Melts Us

The Holy Spirit warms us and melts our cold, cold hearts. Recently, I ran across a parable that makes the point. Once upon a time, there was a piece of iron that was very strong and very hard. Many attempts had been made to break it, but all had failed.

"I'll master it," said the ax. And his blows fell heavily upon the piece of iron, but every blow only made the ax's edge more blunt, until it finally ceased to strike and gave up in frustration.

"Leave it to me," said the saw, and it worked back and forth on the iron's surface until its jagged teeth were all worn and broken. In despair, the saw quit trying and fell to the ground.

"Shall I try?" asked the small soft flame.

"Forget it," everyone else said. "What can you do? You're too small, and you have no strength." But the small soft flame curled around the piece of iron, embraced it, and never stopped until the iron melted under its warm, irresistible influence.

God's way is not to break hearts, but to melt them. And this is our calling—to melt hearts, under the irresistible warmth of God's graciousness. First, the Holy Spirit melts us.

The Holy Spirit Molds Us

The Holy Spirit changes us, shapes us, redeems us. In the early part of this century, an outspoken atheist in London, Charles Bradlaugh, challenged a preacher named Hugh Price Hughes to a public debate. The preacher accepted the challenge with one condition— that he could bring with him to the debate one hundred men and women who would be witnesses of the redeeming love of God and what it can do to the human heart. They would show how God had changed their lives and turned their lives around.

The minister asked his atheist challenger to do the

same thing—bring a group of persons who had been similarly helped by the gospel of atheism. Well, the debate never happened. The preacher was there with his hundred transformed persons, but Bradlaugh, the atheist, never showed up. The proposed debate turned into a worship service, as one by one these Christians shared the good news that through the power of Jesus Christ and the presence of the Holy Spirit, God had melted their hearts and remolded their lives. The Holy Spirit melts us and molds us.

The Holy Spirit Fills Us

The author of a devotion I once read told about the strangest sporting event of them all—the demolition derby. In this crazy event, automobiles race around a track and intentionally crash into each other. The last car moving is declared the winner! He pointed out that when you watch a demolition derby, you discover that many parts of an automobile are not necessary for it to run. Doors, hoods, mirrors, hubcaps litter the track as the derby progresses, and the cars still move.

But one thing is essential—an engine! A car must have power. No power, no movement! In a similar way, we discover in living the Christian life that though discipleship has many parts, many components, there is one essential—the Holy Spirit. The Holy Spirit melts us, molds us, fills us, and enables us to move.

The Holy Spirit Uses Us

In *Who's Coming to Dinner,* Robert Morgan also reminds us that Erasmus, the famous Renaissance scholar, once told a classic story designed to emphasize how important it is that we take up the torch of Christ's ministry with great commitment. In the story, Jesus returns to heaven after his time on earth. The angels gather around him to learn what happened during his days on earth. Jesus tells them of the miracles, his teachings, his death on the cross, and his resurrection.

When he finishes his story, Michael, the Archangel, asks, "But what happens now?"

Jesus answers, "I have left behind eleven faithful disciples, and a handful of men and women who have faithfully followed me. They will declare my message and express my love. The faithful people will build my church."

"But," responds Michael, "what if these people fail? What then is your other plan?"

And Jesus answers, "I have no other plan."

The point is clear, and the message is obvious—Jesus is counting on you and me. Even though there are times when we feel afraid, confused, and overwhelmed, when we feel hard-pressed to face up to the demands, the good news is this: We are not alone! The Holy Spirit is here to melt us, mold us, fill us, and use us.

12.

When You or Someone You Love Faces a Drug Problem

Matthew 25:1-13: Then the kingdom of heaven will be like this. Ten bridesmaids took their lamps and went to meet the bridegroom. Five of them were foolish, and five were wise. When the foolish took their lamps, they took no oil with them; but the wise took flasks of oil with their lamps. As the bridegroom was delayed, all of them became drowsy and slept. But at midnight there was a shout, "Look! Here is the bridegroom! Come out to meet him." Then all those bridesmaids got up and trimmed their lamps. The foolish said to the wise, "Give us some of your oil, for our lamps are going out." But the wise replied, "No! there will not be enough for you and for us; you had better go to the dealers and buy some for yourselves." And while they went to buy it, the bridegroom came, and those who were ready went with him into the wedding banquet; and the door was shut. Later the other bridesmaids came also, saying, "Lord, lord, open to us." But he replied, "Truly I tell you, I do not know you." Keep awake therefore, for you know neither the day nor the hour.

*I*n recent months, the city in which I live has been called "a city under siege"—a city like other large cities of our nation, "under attack." We are facing an evil so dangerous, so insidious, so destructive, that it is threatening our nation and, indeed, our world. I'm talking, of course, about the drug problem, drug abuse. Illegal drugs, and all the horrible baggage that comes with the problem, are tearing the heart out of our nation and our world.

Drug abuse is a problem that affects us all. No one is immune to its effects; its eradication is everyone's responsibility. Did you know that not long ago, drug abuse was considered by many to be a "victimless" crime? But no more: We know better now. We now realize that the consequences of substance abuse are so far-reaching and widespread that they literally transcend generations.

• Did you know that the children of drug-abusing parents are four times more likely to become abusers than the children of nonabusing parents?
• Did you know that 85 percent of crime in the United States today is drug-related—85 percent! And it is increasing every year. Did you know that the crime rate in America has doubled in the last four years, mainly because of drugs?
• Did you know that the cost to our nation for this drug crisis is estimated at $300 billion dollars a year—not to mention what it costs in human lives?
• Did you know that today millions of Americans are participating in drug abuse—using heroin, hallucinogens, inhalants, sedatives, marijuana, and cocaine?
• In addition, millions more are drinking alcohol excessively, making alcohol the single most abused substance in the U.S.
• Did you know that studies reveal that large numbers of high school students have participated in drug abuse? When asked why they were involved in substance abuse, the students cited peer pressure, curiosity, social acceptance, boredom, inadequate laws, and—listen to

this—parental and other adult role models! In many cases, the sources of the abused substances were parents, family members, or family friends.

It is a sad, tragic, unfortunate fact that most young people will at some time be approached, offered, and encouraged to try some illegal drug. We need to get them ready to face that. But it is not just a problem with youth.

• Did you know that eleven is the average age for the first-time drug user in America?
• Did you know that our nation now has the largest demand for, and consumption of, illegal drugs in the history of the world?
• And did you know that the primary cause of drug abuse is low self-esteem? Low self-esteem—this means that the drug problem is more of a spiritual problem than a medical one. This means that we need to strongly cultivate a healthful self-esteem and a firm spiritual strength in our children, in our friends, and in ourselves.

Those most likely to experiment with drugs or get hooked on drugs are those who feel insecure, those who feel not quite able to face up to the stresses of life, those who think they can't have a good time or face a problem or make a decision without some help, some crutch, or some drug. Research has shown that the earlier we begin prevention efforts, the greater the likelihood of lasting success.

I once heard a story about a woman who, after hearing the great minister Dr. Phillips Brooks speak, asked him, "Dr. Brooks, when should I begin to teach faith to my child?"

Dr. Brooks responded, "What age is your child now?"

The woman answered, "She is two years old."

"Hurry home, lady, hurry home," said Phillips Brooks. "You are three years late already!"

What can we do about this tremendous problem? Well, we can support our government and our law-enforcement officials as they try to find new ways and new resources to combat the illegal drug traffic—the supply side of the problem. And we must aggressively attack the demand side of the crisis. Now, I am certainly no authority on the subject of drug abuse, but I believe strongly that it's time for the church to speak out boldly. I don't have any instant answers or magical solutions, but I do have some thoughts to share.

First, a Word About Casual Drug Users

There are lots of those in our country—people who naively still think that drug abuse is a "victimless" crime, that they can smoke marijuana or use other drugs in the privacy of their homes, with no harm to anyone; they think they should have this right. But they are wrong! They are contributing to the problem! They are supporting a spiritual malignancy that is so evil that its tentacles are threatening to strangle the very life out of our world! They are driving up insurance rates and the cost of living. They are participating in and encouraging the increase of criminal activity in our communities. We must plead with them, individually and collectively, to please stop!

Second, a Word About Parents

We must strengthen the family. Whether we are part of a two-parent family or a one-parent family, we must spend more time together as families. We must provide wholesome family activities for our children. Go to the park, see a ball game, go to the theater, have picnics, attend church together as families. What we parents do now will prepare our children to say No to drugs and remain drug-free. Here are some practical tips for parents.

1. Love your children, and let them know how much you love them. Express that love continually in words and deeds.

2. Keep the lines of communication open. Listen to your children. Be interested in them and in what they have to say. Enjoy your children; don't nag at them. Create the kind of atmosphere in which your children feel free to come to you and talk about anything and everything.

3. Know where your children are and what they are doing—and let them know where you are and what you are doing. Mystery is a red flag!

4. Know their friends, and take time to meet their friends' parents.

5. Establish a set of house rules that are clear and fair—and that apply equitably to everyone in the family.

6. Establish curfews for school nights and weekends and special events. Be clear about what is expected, and be awake when your children return home in the evening. Welcome them home and be interested in how the evening went.

7. Talk to your children about the danger of drugs.

Just as you teach them not to play with matches or run into the street, teach them the danger of drugs.

8. Talk to your children about peer pressure. It is one of the main reasons children first experiment with drugs.

9. Know the adversary. Learn about drugs—their names, their uses, their effects on the body. Find out where the drug hangouts are in your community and keep your children away from them. Make them off-limits—and report suspicious activity to the police.

10. And parents, take a good, long, hard look at your own alcohol and prescription medication usage. If you need a drink or a tranquilizer to face every situation, then you've got a problem, and you are sending a bad message to your children. Children learn from what they see and hear—especially at home.

11. Monitor the quality of television programs and movies your children watch. People in the entertainment industry will tell you they don't influence the social climate—they only reflect it. Don't buy that! Don't believe it for a minute! Children and youth especially, but indeed all of us, are affected and influenced more than we can imagine by what we see on TV and in movies.

12. And most important—build your children's self-esteem. Emphasize self-worth and self-respect! Teach independent decision-making! Remind them constantly that they are special—special to you and special to God! Teach them the Christian faith as a life-style! Live the faith before them. Keep them close to the church. Keep them in Sunday school and in worship! Teach them the Scriptures. Teach them to pray. Pray with them. Let them see and hear you pray! And make them dramatically aware of how important God and the church are to you!

A Word About Young People

I know that as young people grow and mature, they want to be free, they want to be independent. I understand that. I know that sometimes the rules seem bothersome, but the following story, I think, makes a good point.

Recently, a family went on a fishing trip together. The two teenage daughters, aged seventeen and nineteen, became bored after a couple of days and wanted to go home. As the two girls pulled onto the interstate to head home, three large trucks pulled alongside them almost immediately and stayed right with them all the way to their hometown, some sixty miles away. The teenagers were annoyed by this. They resented the way the trucks stayed with them so closely.

As they arrived home, the phone was ringing. It was their dad, checking to be sure they had made it home safely. Immediately, the girls began to sputter and complain about the truckers.

But their dad said, "Well, that was my fault. After you left, I got worried about you. You know we've had some trouble with that car, so I broadcast a description of your car on the CB and asked people to watch for you and keep me informed."

Those truckers picked up the call and told him, "We've got them in sight. Don't worry now. We're going to the same town. We'll escort them safely to the city limits and let you know when they are there."

Now, here is the point: What seemed to those teenagers like a bothersome intrusion was actually a symbol of love and caring and protection. Children and youth need to be reminded that the rules are there for their protection. With the rules, parents are really saying, "We care about you! We love you! You are precious to us!"

Also, young people need to be reminded that they have a strong support system in their corner. Parents, family members, friends, ministers, teachers, school counselors—all are there for them and want to help them. And speaking of a strong support system, they need to be reminded that God is on their side. God will be with them and see them through. When problems come, they should know that drugs are not the answer. Drugs do not solve problems. They only make matters worse and create more problems.

Drugs are not cool. They are dangerous and destructive. Faith in Christ is the answer—not drugs! Commitment to the Christian life-style is the answer—not drugs! We must teach our children to say No to drugs and Yes to faith!

Finally, a Word About the Individual Christian

In the parable of the wise and foolish maidens, five were foolish because they ran out of oil at the most crucial moment. They were not prepared, and that lack of preparation came back to haunt them. The point of the parable is a good one and, in my opinion, it relates dramatically to the drug problem.

It tells us to prepare ahead! It tells us that when crises come, we better be prepared, because there are some things we just can't borrow at the last moment. Sometimes we must have the spiritual strength to stand on our own two feet—and that spiritual strength comes only from knowing who we are and whose we are; what we believe and what we are committed to! Spiritual poise, spiritual dedication, spiritual strength—we can't run and borrow that at the last minute. We can't magically produce that at the crucial moment. We have to grow our own, over a long period of time. Rudyard Kipling expressed it powerfully like this:

> If you can keep your head when all about you
>   Are losing theirs and blaming it on you,
> If you can trust yourself when all men doubt you,
>   But make allowance for their doubting too;
> If you can wait and not be tired by waiting,
>   Or being lied about, don't deal in lies;
> Or being hated don't give way to hating,
>   And yet don't look too good, nor talk too wise:
>
> If you can dream—and not make dreams your master;
>   If you can think—and not make thoughts your aim:
> If you can meet with Triumph and Disaster
>   And treat those two imposters just the same;
> If you can bear to hear the truth you've spoken
>   Twisted by knaves to make a trap for fools,
> Or watch the things you gave your life to, broken,
>   And then stoop down and build 'em up again
>   with worn-out tools.

Spiritual poise, spiritual maturity, spiritual strength—that's what it takes to face the crisis moment. That's what it takes to stand firmly against the menace of drugs. It comes only after hours and hours of preparation, hours and hours of fellowship with God and God's people.

13.

When You're So Tired You Want to Give Up

II Timothy 4:6-8: As for me, I am already being poured out as a libation, and the time of my departure has come. I have fought the good fight, I have finished the race, I have kept the faith. From now on there is reserved for me the crown of righteousness, which the Lord, the righteous judge, will give me on that day, and not only to me but also to all who have longed for his appearing.

*S*ome years ago when I was in high school, I enjoyed running track. I ran the 100-meter dash, the 200-meter dash, and also took part in some of the field events like the long jump and the high jump. But what I really got a kick out of was being on the sprint relay teams.

There was something very special to me about being part of a team—the spirit, the fellowship, the community—the closeness that comes from working together like a well-tuned synchronized machine; the unique family feeling that comes from winning and losing together, from rejoicing and hurting together, from laughing and crying together.

Now, we had an outstanding 800-meter relay team my senior year. There were four of us. Each runner would run 200 meters and hand off the baton at full speed to the next man, who would then run his leg of the race and pass the baton to the next, until the team had completed the 800-meter distance. Throughout the track season that spring, we had done very well. We had come through all our meets undefeated—right up to the day of the regional meet.

All we had to do was finish in the top three to win a trip to the state meet. Needless to say, we were confident—maybe even a little cocky. We had already made our plans for our trip. Then came the time for the race, the 800-meter relay. We were primed and ready!

Our first runner quickly jumped out in front and gave us a good lead. Our second runner ran well and increased our lead. I was running third, and when I passed the baton to our anchor man, we had a fifty-yard lead. I thought to myself, "We've got it won. There's no way they can catch us now!"

As I watched our last runner coming out of the final turn, way in front, I began to think about the medals we were going to win, the trophy with our names on it that would be placed in the trophy case at school, our pictures in the morning paper, the trip and the opportunity to run in the state track meet.

But then suddenly, I was brought back to reality. Just twenty-five yards short of the finish line, our anchorman pulled a muscle and fell down! As he lay there, holding his leg and writhing in pain, one by one, the other runners passed him. And instead of first place, we came in last—dead last! That quickly, it was all over! I can remember as if it were yesterday, the sick feeling in the pit of my stomach—concern and empathy for my injured teammate, hurt and disappointment over our lost opportunity.

But you know, I learned a valuable lesson that day. I learned how important it is to finish what we start—to bring it to conclusion! It's not enough to make a good start. It's not enough to run well most of the way. We must finish what we start. We must see it through, or it is all of no avail! Harry Emerson Fosdick said it well:

> A very serious test of human fiber is involved in the fact that there are so many good beginnings and poor endings. . . .
>
> Good starters and good stayers are not necessarily the same people. Ardor, excitement . . . the flare of good intentions—such forces set men going, but they do not enable men to carry on when the going is hard. That requires another kind of moral energy which evidently is not so common as the first. Plenty of people are equipped with efficient self-starters. They get away easily. They are off with fleet eagerness . . . but they peter out; they soon stick in the sand or stall on a high hill. . . .
>
> In one of our Federal prisons today is a man who for fifty years with unblemished reputation lived a life of probity and honor in his own community. Then, as a government servant, he went to France . . . and mishandled funds. Only that will be remembered about him. The half century of fine living is blotted out. He was not able to finish. (*Twelve Tests of Character,* pp. 199-200)

In the United States, we have seen it close at hand—in the religious arena, on the political scene—highly regarded leaders faltered and faded, unable to see it through! Against this backdrop, it becomes more meaningful to hear the apostle Paul say, "I have fought the good fight; I have kept the faith; I have finished the course." Against this backdrop, the words of Jesus ring out even more powerfully as we see him hanging on the cross, saying with his last breath, "It is finished!" I have seen it through.

All through life, and in every field, we see the importance of this kind of determination and perseverance.

We See It in History

The great people of history were those who had the power to see it through, with determination, commitment, and tenacity—they persisted, they endured, they persevered. Let me show you some examples.

• **ALBERT EINSTEIN**—When he was in grade school, he was considered a poor student.

When his father asked the headmaster what profession young Albert should pursue, the headmaster replied, "It really doesn't matter, because he will never make a success of anything." But Einstein went on to become one of the great intellectuals of the twentieth century, and probably the greatest physicist of all time—more because of determined persistence than because of easy genius. He had the power to see it through.

• **WINSTON CHURCHILL**—In school, he too was a slow student. As a public servant, it seemed to be all over for him in the 1930s, since he had failed to achieve most of his dreams and goals. But he stayed alert and alive. He hung on, and later at age sixty-six, when a rare opportunity for leadership came, he was ready. At a time when most folks retire, Winston Churchill became the British Prime Minister and was a source of strength, confidence, and inspiration—not only for his own country, but for all the western world. Because of his power to see it through with bulldog-like tenacity, he came to be regarded by many as the greatest political leader of the twentieth century.

• **ABRAHAM LINCOLN**—From 1830 through 1860, a thirty-year period, he had all kinds of problems,

116

defeats, and difficulties, but he refused to quit. Twice he failed in business; he had a nervous breakdown; he ran for political office eight times and lost. Finally in 1860, he won. He was elected president of the United States—and you know the rest of the story.

• **FRANKLIN D. ROOSEVELT**—He was president of the United States longer than any other person. Severely crippled by polio, he served all those dramatic years through depression and war in a wheelchair. As you recall, one of his great strengths was his public speaking, at a time when the radio had given direct access to all the American people.

Those famous "fireside chats" sounded informal and off-the-cuff. But at Hyde Park, New York, there is a glass case which displays nine drafts of one of Roosevelt's famous speeches. The first draft was rough; the second improved; the third showed still greater improvement. And only one word was changed in the eighth draft before the ninth and final draft was run. What sounded so casual and matter-of-fact was really the result of arduous, painstaking hard work and perseverance. Roosevelt was another who had the power to see it through.

• **HELEN KELLER**—She was doomed to defeat, unable to see, unable to hear, unable to communicate, yet she became an inspiration to the whole world because she had the power to see it through.

• **ADMIRAL ROBERT E. PERRY**—He was determined to reach the North Pole and claim it for the United States. Seven times he started out; seven times he failed. The eighth time, after incredible hardships, he made it. After twenty-three years of trying, at the age of fifty-three, he reached it!

We See It in the World of Sports

• **LEE TREVINO**—Some years ago, he was a poor caddy at a wind-blown golf course in El Paso, Texas. When he had no golf clubs, he made his own. He wrapped tape around a soft-drink bottle attached to the end of a stick—and beat everybody in sight. Through determination, he became one of the most beloved, respected, popular, and successful professional golfers of all time. Even now, he frequently goes to the driving range after a tournament to perfect a single shot by practicing two or three hundred times, until his hands are bruised and blistered. He has the power to see it through.

• **TOM DEMPSEY**—Tom holds the National Football League record for the longest field goal—a kick of sixty-five yards. It's significant to note that Tom Dempsey was born with half an arm and half a foot. The half-foot is the one with which he kicks!

We See It in the Scientific Laboratory

• **THOMAS EDISON**—He tried 586 experiments before he found the right filament for the light bulb.

During that process, his assistant said, "It's a shame to have tried 586 times and failed!"

Quick as a wink, Edison replied, "We do not have 586 failures. We have 586 victories! We now know 586 things that won't work!" He refused to be defeated. He had the power to see it through, to finish what he started.

Again and Again, We Find It in the Scriptures

We see it most dramatically in Jesus. If ever anyone had a difficult conclusion to face, it was Jesus. Yet if he had given up in Gethsemane, unable to finish, all his teaching would have been forgotten, all his works of mercy would have been lost to our memories, and everything he had done and said and stood for, up to that moment, would have been wasted. His victory lay in his power to say at Calvary: "It is finished!" I have completed it! I have seen it through!

Then, too, how about the apostle Paul. If ever a man might have been tempted to give up, it was Paul. Yet, if he had collapsed in prison in despair, unable to finish, his fine start on the Damascus Road, all his eloquent preaching, all he stood for, would have gone for nothing. Paul's life and faith gave him the power to finish, the power to see it through, the power to turn the prisoner's dock into a pulpit, his prison cell into a publishing house for the New Testament.

And later he could say, "I have fought the good fight. I have kept the faith. I have finished the course." In *Faith for a Nuclear Age*, J. Wallace Hamilton relates a story he heard from a German author:

Once upon a time in the development of life . . . the birds had no wings. They crawled about in the grass like squirrels and mice and other earth-bound creatures. . . . Then one day the Lord threw wings at their feet and commanded them to pick them up and carry them. At first it seemed very hard. The little birds didn't want

119

them—those heavy, unwieldy things. But they loved the Lord, and in obedience, they picked up the heavy things, carried them on their backs, and lo, the wings fastened there. Finally the little birds caught on to it, that what they had once thought would be a hampering weight became the means by which they were released into the freedom of the sky. (pp. 79, 80)

That is precisely what the New Testament tells us about our burdens and the things that happen to us. First, we carry them, and then they begin to carry us to higher altitudes of life. Our burdens can become wings for us if we refuse to quit, if we won't give up. If we do the best we can and trust God, we will be given the strength, the confidence, and the courage, and God will give us the power to see it through!

14.

When Your Faith Lands on the Critical List

Mark 14:32-36: They went to a place called
Gethsemane; and he said to his disciples, "Sit here
while I pray." He took with him Peter and James
and John, and began to be distressed and agitated.
And he said to them, "I am deeply grieved, even to
death; remain here, and keep awake." And going a
little farther, he threw himself on the ground and
prayed that, if it were possible, the hour might pass
from him. He said, "Abba, Father, for you all
things are possible; remove this cup from me; yet,
not what I want, but what you want."

There is a story about a very tough old westerner
who walked in one morning to visit the town
blacksmith. Now it so happened that the blacksmith had
just pulled a red-hot horseshoe out of the fire and laid it
to one side to cool. It had cooled just enough so that it
wasn't red anymore, but it was still really hot. The tough
westerner, not knowing the horseshoe was hot, reached
over and picked it up. Then he quickly threw it down,
stuck his hand in his pants pocket, and began to whistle.

The blacksmith said, "Did you burn your hand?"

The westerner answered, "No. It just doesn't take me
very long to look at a horseshoe!"

Now, we often treat some of these great Scripture pas-
sages like that. We pick them up, look at them quickly,
and toss them aside. Let us look at this powerful passage in Mark 14 . . .

. . . a little more intentionally,
. . . a little more carefully,
. . . a little more in depth.

Jesus is praying and agonizing in the Garden of Gethsemane.

"Abba, Father," he prays, "for you all things are possible; remove this cup from me; yet, not what I want, but what you want." There is much to learn here about faith and about how to keep our faith alive. That is a very basic and significant question, isn't it? How do we keep our faith alive? "O for a faith that will not shrink"—that is what one old hymn pleads. The hymn writer knew about this problem many people seem to have in their spiritual experience.

It happens far too much and far too often. People have a meaningful "faith experience." They become excited, enthusiastic, devoted, committed. Every time the church doors open, they are there. They can't wait to get there. The whole new world of faith has opened up to them, and it's all too wonderful for words. For several weeks or months—sometimes even years—all goes well. They have no problem with their faith. But suddenly they begin to have difficulties. They begin to drop out . . .

. . . the luster wears off,
. . . the excitement wears thin,
. . . their enthusiasm wears down,
. . . their devotional commitment shrinks.

And after a while, they disappear and become not much more than names on a church roll somewhere. No one sees them at church anymore. No one really seems to know them anymore.

Why does this happen? And how can we prevent it?

How can we keep our spiritual experience vibrant and zestful? How can we keep our faith alive and well?

Interestingly, we can find some fascinating and helpful clues in the Garden of Gethsemane. Ironically, when we look closely at Jesus as he faces the prospect of physical death, we find the keys to staying spiritually alive. Let me show you what I mean as I list four keys, or four ingredients, of a lively, healthy faith.

To Keep Our Faith Alive, We Must Continue to Pray

It is so important to have a good prayer life in your faith experience. Jesus was a man of prayer. We notice in the Gospels that he often "went apart" to pray. Every time I hear that, I think, "If Jesus needed to pray, how much more do we!" It was his way of communing with God, so we are not surprised that he fell on his knees in the Garden of Gethsemane. It was the most natural thing in the world for him to do.

This was a tough, terrible moment. The cross loomed before him. He didn't want to go to the cross. He prayed about it: "Father . . . remove this cup from me." It was an earnest prayer. The King James version puts it dramatically—it says that he sweated drops of blood! This is serious business here! That's how difficult it was in that moment to pray. It was agony, but pray he did.

And somehow, in that prayer experience, he found the strength to say, "Not what I want, but what you want. Thy will be done, Father, not mine"!

Prayer was his means of keeping his faith alive. It kept him in touch with God, and because of it, he was able to do what he had to do. There's an old spiritual that says, "Not my brother, not my sister, but it's me, O Lord, standing in the need of prayer." We all need it. Prayer is conversation with God; prayer is friendship with God. It's the way we keep the lines of communication open between ourselves and our Lord. The truth is that if we don't pray, our relationship with God will fade, and our faith will shrink and shrivel and die.

It's like an experience I had with a childhood friend. We went through school together—grammar school, junior high, and high school. We were real buddies. We walked to school together almost every day, we played ball together, we worked together. Once we even studied together! We did everything together. We were close. We knew each other so well that sometimes we knew what was going on in the other's mind.

But then we graduated. He went to work and I went away to college. The four years of college passed, and I went further away to seminary. We lost contact. There was no communication between us. We didn't see each other, didn't write, didn't talk on the phone; and when we met again, we discovered that we were not the same. The relationship was not the same. It was awkward.

- We were like strangers.
- We had trouble holding a conversation.
- We didn't really feel comfortable with each other anymore.
- We no longer felt close, because we had lost contact.

Once we had been so close, like brothers. Now we were virtual strangers. Why? Because we had not been communicating.

This same kind of thing can happen in our relationship with God. If we do not pray, we find our relationship with God growing dimmer and weaker. One of our problems with prayer is that we mistakenly think it requires a special kind of "holy-sounding language" that boasts of "pious phrases" and "pontifical tones"—and nothing could be further from the truth!

Prayer is friendship with God, conversation with God. We don't need a special language or a sanctimonious tone to talk to a friend. All we need to talk with God is a willingness to communicate with him and to be in his presence.

A short time before he died, the great comedian Jack Benny appeared on the "Tonight Show."

He turned to Johnny Carson and, in his unique way, said, "You know, the other night I dreamed about God, and God said to me, 'Jack' "—here Benny stopped with that characteristic long pause, then added, "You know, God knows practically everybody!" It is mind-boggling to realize that we have a God who is on a first-name basis with each of us and wants to spend time with us.

If we can come at prayer like that, remembering that God is our friend, it helps so much. A friend is one with whom we can share our joys and sorrows, our victories and our defeats, our confidences and our worries, our deepest thoughts and lightest wonderings.

We can do that, can't we? In fact, we need to do it to keep our faith alive. If we don't pray, if we don't communicate with God, our faith will shrink and shrivel and die.

We Must Continue to Grow and Learn

We must continue to study and think. In the Garden of Gethsemane, Jesus was open to new truth. His mind was working overtime, straining, stretching, struggling—no closed-mindedness here. He didn't say, "Now, see here, this is the way it is and there is no other way!" He didn't say, "Now, wait a minute, Father, we never did it that way before!" No, he was open to God's truth, he was open to God's will, he was open to God's direction.

Being a disciple means being a learner. Too often and too quickly, people forget that and close their minds. There is a story about a little boy who fell out of bed one night. He said, "I guess I fell asleep too close to where I first got in!"

This can happen to us. We can fall asleep too close to where we first got in, and consequently, we drop out. The tragedy is that as soon as we stop studying and learning and growing in the faith, at that moment, our faith begins to shrivel and fade, shrink and die. We are like plants, in that we need "light" to grow. To keep our faith alive, we must continue to pray and grow and study and think and learn.

We Must Continue to Obey God

"Christian obedience," we call it. When Jesus left the Garden of Gethsemane, he went out to climb the cross. Note that he didn't want to do it. That was not his first choice. He struggled against it. He agonized over it—but he did it! He did it because he knew that he must stand tall for what is right; he knew that he must not run away. He knew that he had to strike a blow for God's justice, even if it meant death on a cross.

If I were to ask you what one word would best describe Jesus, the overriding quality of Jesus' life, what would you say? Most of us would probably say *love*— and rightly so—but a very close second key ingredient of his life was *obedience.* "Not what I want, but what you want"—that was the prayer-theme of his life.

To keep our faith alive, we need that brand of commitment, that kind of come-what-may obedience. All the great people of faith have it. John Bunyan had been thrown in prison for preaching. After a long time, he was told that if he would stop preaching about Christ, he would be released.

John Bunyan answered, "I am determined yet to suffer till moss grows over my eyebrows, rather than violate my faith."

"Fair-weather faith" will not survive. The only kind of faith that will not shrink and shrivel and die is faith rooted in Christlike obedience—a thy-will-be-done obedience!

We Must Be Determined to Stay with It, No Matter What

We need prayer, we need growth, we need obedience, and we need determination. In the Garden of Gethsemane, Jesus had every reason to drop out. It would have been easy to "go over the hill" or throw in the towel, but he would not quit. He had made up his mind to do the best he knew and to trust God to bring it out right. Later, on the cross, he said it: "Father, into your hands, I commit my spirit." Wouldn't that be a great prayer for us to pray every morning? "Father, today, into your hands I commit my spirit." Keeping our faith alive takes determination and perseverance. It takes a come-what-may, an I- will-not-quit kind of attitude!

I heard of a corporate sales manager who got up before all two thousand of his firm's salespeople and said, "Did the Wright brothers ever quit?"

The salesforce shouted, "No!"

Then he yelled out, "Did Charles Lindbergh ever quit?"

Again, the salespeople shouted, "No!"

He yelled out a third time, "Did Joan of Arc ever quit?"

The salespeople, warming to the moment, shouted back even louder, "No!"

Finally, he bellowed out a fourth time, "Did Thorndyke McKeester ever quit?" There was a long silence.

Finally one lone brave man stood up and said it for all of them: "Sir, forgive me for asking, but who's Thorndyke McKeester? We never heard of him."

The sales manager snapped back, "Of course you never heard of him, because he quit!"

Now, in the early church, there was a leader who was a close friend of the apostle Paul, a co-worker with Paul. He was talented, bright, capable, full of potential, but I would venture to say that most of you have never heard of him—because he quit! His name was Demas. In II Timothy 4:10, we find these haunting words: "Demas . . . has deserted." He was destined for greatness, but he got lost in the shuffle, simply because he quit!

Let me tell you something, with all the feeling I have in my heart: Please don't quit! Don't quit on life! Don't quit on the church! Don't quit on God! It's true with most everything, isn't it? You have to make up your mind to stay with it! And nowhere is that more true than in the faith pilgrimage. It takes a lot of prayer, a lot of growth, a lot of obedience, and a whole lot of determination to keep our faith alive. Oh for a faith that will not shrink!

15.

When a Healing Word Is Needed

Matthew 8:5-8, 10, 13: When he entered Capernaum, a centurion came to him, appealing to him, and saying, "Lord, my servant is lying at home paralyzed, in terrible distress." And he said to him, "I will come and cure him." The centurion answered, "Lord, I am not worthy to have you come under my roof; but only speak the word, and my servant will be healed." . . .

When Jesus heard him, he was amazed and said to those who followed him, "Truly I tell you, in no one in Israel have I found such faith." . . .

And to the centurion Jesus said, "Go; let it be done for you according to your faith." And the servant was healed in that hour.

*I*n one of the "Peanuts" comic strips, Charlie Brown receives a surprise telephone call from a secret admirer.

She says, "Charlie Brown, this is your secret admirer. I want you to know that I think you are charming, dashing, and wonderful. I am leaving for camp this afternoon and while I'm there, I will think of you every minute. I will miss you, Charlie Brown, and I will look forward to seeing your handsome face when I return. I love you!" And then she hangs up.

Charlie Brown, the perennial loser, stands there by the phone, absolutely stunned, with this incredible grin on his face.

"Who was that?" asks Linus.

129

Still grinning broadly, Charlie Brown says, "I don't know, but I think it was a right number!"

Now, the message of that cartoon is clear: Words are powerful! The right words, spoken at the right time, by the right person, have the amazing ability to lift us up, to inspire us, to motivate us, to affirm us, to invigorate us—indeed, even to heal us. Just think of that. When we are down and out, words have the power to bring healing.

In *The Healing Heart,* Norman Cousins told a story that makes the point dramatically. A man was in the hospital, seriously ill, with a severe heart problem. Each day he became weaker and weaker.

Then one morning, he overheard his doctor tell the attending staff that this patient had a "third-sound gallop" in his heart. Now, as I understand it, a "third-sound gallop" is a very poor sign and denotes that the heart muscle is straining and usually failing. Strangely, however, this patient (quite unexpectedly) suddenly began to improve, and a short time later was discharged from the hospital.

Some months later, the man's doctor, amazed at his incredible recovery, asked him if he could recall anything that had happened that might explain the marvelous turnaround.

The man answered, "Doctor, I not only know what got me better, but even the exact moment when it happened. I was sure the end was near and that you and your staff had given up hope. However, that Thursday morning when you entered with your troops, something happened that changed everything.

"You listened to my heart; you seemed pleased by the findings, and you announced to all those standing about my bed that my heart had a 'wholesome gallop.' I knew that in talking to me, you doctors might try to soften things. But I knew you wouldn't kid each other, so when I overheard you tell your colleagues that I had a wholesome gallop, I just figured my heart still had a lot of kick, so I could not be dying. My spirits were lifted, and I knew that I would recover."

Isn't that something? The astonishing power of words to bring healing! That's what this Scripture lesson in Matthew is all about. A Roman centurion comes to Jesus and asks him to heal his servant with words: "Just say the word and my servant will be healed."

Jesus was touched by the extraordinary compassion of this Roman centurion, because at that time many masters were quite ruthless with their slaves. They often treated them like inanimate objects, using them up, and when they became unable to work, they discarded them casually—sometimes even brutally.

But this centurion obviously loved his servant as if he were a member of the family. He was deeply grieved over his illness and was determined to do everything he could to help him.

Jesus was impressed, and he said, "I will come and cure him."

But the centurion answered, "Lord, I am not worthy to have you come under my roof; but only speak the word, and my servant will be healed."

Jesus was moved by his faith: "Go, let it be done for you according to your faith." And the servant was healed. End of story.

Now, at this point we could go off in several different directions. We could examine the great faith of this Roman centurion, a faith so strong that it impressed Jesus. Or we could discuss the marvelous capacity of Jesus to bridge the gap between different nations, even between Jews and Romans. Or we could look at the awesome ability of Jesus to heal people—even long distance. But for now, let me invite you to zero in on the

131

healing power of words—"Only say the words and healing will come."

Of course, we all know that Jesus could speak the words of healing. But on a lesser level, in a different dimension, yet in a significant way—so can we! This is the calling to all Christians: We are called to continue the preaching, teaching, caring, healing ministry of Christ! And one way we can do that is through the sacred task of speaking those powerful words that can bring healing to hurt hearts, that can bring wholeness to broken and grieving spirits.

We Can Speak the Words of Empathy

Empathy is a great word, and it implies an even greater spirit than the word *sympathy*. Let me define these two words like this: *Sympathy* means to feel sorry *for* somebody; *empathy* means to feel sorry *with* somebody. It's to feel another's hurt, to experience another's pain, to walk in another's shoes.

I love the old story about the little girl who was late coming home from school one day.

When her mother asked why she was late, the little girl said, "My friend Nancy was sad because her puppy died today. And I stayed to help."

"How did you help?" asked the mom.

And the little girl replied, "I helped her cry!"

That is precisely what *empathy* is. It's helping people cry, sharing their pain, hurting with them, holding their hand as they walk through the hard valleys of life.

Jesus was a master at that. Immediately, he could tune in to the heartache of others. He could feel the deep loneliness of Zacchaeus when he saw him perched in that sycamore tree. He could recognize the significance of that sick woman's timid touch at the hem of his garment. There was something special about that touch . . . and he sensed it. He could feel and share in the pain of those people, and because of that, he knew just the right words, the empathetic words that bring healing.

Some years ago, Millie McWhorter wrote *Hushed Were the Hills,* in which she shares her childhood experiences in Tennessee. In one of her stories, she tells about a boy named Joe, who moves to town and comes to the little country school. Joe's father has a terrible problem with drinking, and his reputation spreads through the community like wildfire.

The children are told by their parents to "stay away from Joe. He's the son of that drunkard! Have nothing to do with him." So all the children at school avoid Joe. No one speaks to him, no one reaches out to him, no one befriends him—except Billy Bob Person. Billy Bob shares his lunch with Joe and tries to include Joe in the games at recess.

One day Joe clashed with the teacher and was sent to the cloak room to sit alone in the darkness. After a while, the teacher noticed that Billy Bob was missing. When she asked the class, "Where is Billy Bob?" no one seemed to know—or at least they weren't telling. Billy Bob had not asked to be excused, nor had he gone outside, and he was too big to be hiding in the room. There was only one place he could be.

The teacher walked to the door of the cloak room, opened the door, and called out, "Billy Bob Person, are you in there?" She could see him sitting there on the bench by Joe.

"Yes'm," he answered, and Billy Bob and Joe came to the door. The class watched in silence.

Then Billy Bob looked at the teacher with his wide blue eyes and said, "He was in solitary, Miss Wilkins, so I sat with him. That's all I did, honest. I just sat there in the dark with him and talked to him a little bit. Honest, that's all I did."

But that's not all Billy Bob did. He cared. He reached out. He empathized. And that's the spirit of Christ, the spirit we need as Christian people, the spirit we need in the church, the spirit that can, through the miracle of God's grace, bring healing to people who are hurting. We need lots of Billy Bobs, people who can feel the pain of others when they have to walk through the darkness, people who will go through the darkness with them. "Only say the words of empathy and healing will come."

We Can Speak the Words of Love

It has been documented time and again that love promotes healing. When we see people hurting and we want to help them, the best thing we can do is let them know that we love them—speak the words of love.

If you are an ardent football fan, you will remember the close finish at the Super Bowl in 1991. The New York Giants beat the Buffalo Bills by a single point. But remember, Buffalo almost won the game in the final seconds. They had a chance to win. With four seconds on the clock, Scott Norwood attempted a forty-seven-yard field goal. A successful kick would have won the game for Buffalo.

The ball was high enough and it was long enough, but it was wide by only a few feet—and the Bills lost the game. Scott Norwood took it hard. He felt that he had lost the game for his team, for his coaches, and for the thousands of loyal fans back home.

The next day when the Buffalo team returned to their city, more than 25,000 people turned out to cheer them and welcome them home. They cheered the coach. They cheered the team. They cheered the quarterback. But most of all, they cheered Scott Norwood! The chant went up: "We love Scott! We love Scott!" Finally, in a moment charged with deep emotion, Scott Norwood stepped to the microphone.

In a voice breaking with pain, he said, "I've got to tell you that I'm struggling with this right now. But I know that I'm going to make it through this, because I have never felt more loved than I do at this moment." Those words of love, those chants of love, were an important part of the healing process for Scott Norwood.

In December of 1979, my mother was killed in a car wreck. When we returned home from the funeral, we sat down and went through the mail. There were so many beautiful cards, letters, telegrams, and notes from people, expressing their love and sympathy. One of those letters, I will never forget. It was only five words long, but it said it all: "Caring, I share your sorrow." That's all it said—just one sentence long, with only five words: "Caring, I share your sorrow." That letter, and all the rest of those expressions of love, touched our family deeply. They became instruments of God's healing for our broken hearts. Only say the words of empathy and love, and healing will come.

We Can Speak the Words of Encouragement

Rod Wilmoth is a pastor in Nebraska. Recently, he told me about a poignant experience he had this past summer here in Texas. He had gone to a church in a county-seat town in east Texas for a lecture series.

The pastor of the host church has a very special son named Dolph (short for Rudolph). Dolph is twenty-seven years old, but he still lives at home with his parents because he was born with Down's Syndrome. Dolph is an absolute delight, a joy to his family and to his church. He has a job which he handles very well. He sings in the choir and has a marvelous sense of humor. And he is very matter-of-fact about his condition.

For example, one day as they were driving to church, Dolph said, "Dad, I wish I could drive a car."

His father's answer was kind and gentle: "But, Dolph, you know why you can't drive, don't you?"

Dolph said, "Yes, because I'm Down's Syndrome, and in the state of Texas, I can't get a license."

When Rod Wilmoth had finished the lecture there was a question and answer session, and Dolph asked an interesting question: "Rod, do you think if Jesus saw me, he would see someone who is not normal? Would he see someone with Down's Syndrome?" A great hush fell over the hall.

Rod said, "Dolph, I believe that Jesus would see what I see. When I look at you, I do not see someone with Down's Syndrome. I see a wonderful, delightful child of God."

Dolph, beaming, then responded with a statement that carried the day: "I know just what you mean, Rod, because when I receive communion and see the hands of my dad giving me the bread, I look up and I do not see my dad. Instead, I see the face of Jesus."

Has anyone ever looked at you like that? Has anyone ever sensed the presence of Christ in you? When we, in the Spirit of Christ, speak the words of encouragement, people may well see the face of Jesus in us. In the Spirit of Christ, only say the words—the words of empathy, of love, of encouragement—and healing will come. If we will say the words, God will bring the healing.

16.

The Healing Power of Love

John 15: 1-17 *:* "This is my commandment, that you love one another as I have loved you. No one has greater love than this, to lay down one's life for one's friends. You are my friends if you do what I command you. I do not call you servants any longer, because the servant does not know what the master is doing; but I have called you friends, because I have made known to you everything that I have heard from my Father. You did not choose me but I chose you. And I appointed you to go and bear fruit, fruit that will last, so that the Father will give you whatever you ask him in my name. I am giving you these commands so that you may love one another."

There is nothing in the world more powerful than love. Sometimes we forget that or wonder about it—maybe even doubt it. We want to put our faith in military power and economic strength and international alliances and political clout. But again and again, the scriptures tell us that love is the answer, that love is the will of God for us, that love is the single most authentic sign of discipleship, that love is the hope of the world. Here in John 15, we see it again.

Jesus says, "This is my commandment, that you love one another as I have loved you. No one has greater love than this, to lay down one's life for one's friends. . . . I am giving you these commands so that you may love one another." Jesus was the Great Physician, and he knew full well about the healing power of love. That's what I want us to understand—the incredible, amazing, awesome, healing power of love.

Karl Menninger, the well-known psychiatrist, recently said that he believes that the most tragic word in human language today is the word *unloved*. Feeling unloved—there's nothing worse than that, nothing more devastating, nothing more destructive. Dr. Menninger went on to say that, on the other hand, "Love has the power to cure . . . both the ones who give it and the ones who receive it." And he's right. Love can cure. Love can restore and mend and heal. Let me be more specific.

Love Has the Power to Heal Us Physically

Scientific research is now confirming what many of us have suspected all along—that love plays a big part in the healing of a hurting body.

Years ago, someone told me a story about a particularly affectionate puppy that liked to hang around a sanitarium. A doctor at the sanitarium decided to try an experiment with the pup. She made a small incision on the puppy's leg and bandaged it. Then she instructed those at the sanitarium to feed the puppy when he was hungry, but not to show him any affection, either physically or verbally.

The change in the little dog was quick and dramatic. Whereas before, he had always been energetic, frisky, happy, and friendly, he now seemed quite forlorn and pitiful. Even more significantly, six weeks later, the incision on his leg still had not healed. The doctor then instructed everyone at the sanitarium to do just the opposite—to lavish love on the little puppy, speak kindly to him, hold him, pet him, stroke him, love him.

Amazingly, soon the puppy was frisky and happy and energetic again. And the incision healed very quickly. The point is clear: The healing streams that lie within the body, and which may be energized and activated by the power of love, are potent indeed—perhaps more potent than we even realize.

A few years ago in Sweden, a nurse in a government hospital was assigned an older woman patient. This patient was a tough case. She had not spoken a word in three years. Most of the nurses disliked her and tried to avoid her as much as they could. Basically, they ignored her. But the new nurse decided to try "unconditional love."

The woman patient rocked all day in a rocking chair, so one day the nurse pulled a rocking chair up beside the woman and rocked along with her. Occasionally, the nurse would reach over and gently pat the hand of the older woman.

After just a few days of this, the patient suddenly opened her eyes, turned, and said to the nurse, "You're so kind." The next day, she talked some more, and incredibly, two weeks later the woman was well enough to leave the hospital and go home. Of course, it doesn't always work like that, but studies are accumulating which show that, without question, love has healing power.

The poet Elizabeth Barrett was an invalid for many years, unable even to lift her head from her pillow. But one day she was visited by a man named Robert Browning. It was love at first sight, and in just one visit, he brought her so much joy and happiness that she lifted her head. On the second visit, she sat up. On the third visit, they eloped!

Love can heal us physically! No wonder people were healed by coming into physical contact with Jesus. He was love incarnate, and that's what he is calling us to be today—love made flesh, love personified, love lived out. Love can heal bodies; love can heal physically.

Love Has the Power to Heal Us Emotionally

Some years ago when I was serving a church in another state, a man and woman came to see me. It was obvious that they were burdened, worried, troubled. I could tell that both had been crying.

The man spoke first: "It's our daughter, Betty. She's eighteen years old now, and we are worried sick about her. She has absolutely no self-esteem at all, and she has gotten a reputation around town."

"Reputation?" I asked. "What do you mean?"

"Well," said the man painfully, "her self-esteem is so low that whenever any man pays attention to her" . . . his voice trailed off and he began to sob.

Then the woman said bluntly: "Jim, she can't say no to any man, and now she has this horrible reputation. It's all over town! We're worried sick, and we're scared. We're at the end of our rope. We don't know what to do with her. She's emotionally ill. She needs help."

Well, I met with Betty, and they were right about her self-esteem. It was nonexistent. She walked all slumped over. Her hair was dirty and scraggly, her clothes unkempt and out of style. She wore no makeup. She could not look me in the eye. Most of the time she stared at the floor, and when she did look up, her eyes darted like those of a scared rabbit. She was in a pitiful state. I finally brought in a psychiatrist, and we both worked with her. But to be honest, we didn't make much progress at all. It seemed hopeless.

But then the most amazing thing happened. A new young man moved to town, and he fell in love with Betty.

He said, "Betty, I know about your past. I know about your reputation. I know the names they call you. I've heard all the rumors, but I also know that I love you and you are so beautiful to me!"

He kept telling her that: "I love you and you are so beautiful," and pretty soon, she started to believe him. She began to stand up straight. She put on a little makeup and combed her hair. She bought some new clothes. And she did something else I'd never seen her do before—she started smiling! And not long afterward, I performed their wedding.

A few years later, I saw that young couple again. First I saw the husband, and with him was a lovely woman. She looked like a model—tall, stately, poised, radiant. And suddenly I realized that this beautiful woman was Betty! She was gorgeous. She had been transformed. She had been restored. She had been made well. She had been healed by love! Love has the power to heal, both physically and emotionally.

Love Has the Power to Heal Us Spiritually

When I attended a conference in Singapore a few years ago, one of the evening programs was a celebration of Christianity in Asia. It was a magnificent experience as each Asian country in turn came forward, dressed in their native costumes, to share the gospel and the work of the church in their nation. Some sang, some danced, some played instruments, some showed slides. Some did all of the above. It was colorful, majestic, and moving.

141

But for me the highlight of the evening was what happened outside the convention hall in one of the lobbies. A group of fifty children from Singapore, many of them preschoolers, all dressed in costume, were lined up waiting to go in to sing. Their leader was giving them last-minute instructions. They were listening attentively and respectfully, when suddenly on the other side of the door, inside the conference hall, the service started with a hymn, "Amazing Grace."

When those children heard the people singing "Amazing Grace," they became so excited, even though they were outside in the hallway, they started to sing. They belted out "Amazing Grace" in English with gusto. They knew every single word, and they sang it with strength and confidence and joy. Their director only smiled and sang along with them.

It was such a touching moment—to watch and hear those little Asian children sing, and to see the look on their faces. I thought not only about the incredible impact of that hymn on people all across the globe, but about the impact, indeed, of the spiritual healing that God's amazing grace has brought to people of every nation and every race and every culture and every age—all across the face of this earth. The truth is that we can be healed spiritually only by God's amazing grace:

> Amazing grace! How sweet the sound
> that saved a wretch like me!
> I once was lost, but now am found;
> was blind, but now I see.

Spiritual healing, redemption, atonement, salvation—whatever we may call it—comes only from God's gracious love, a love so deep and so powerful that it goes all the way to the cross and dies for you and me.

The Old Testament puts it like this: "By his stripes we are healed." The New Testament says: "For God so loved the world that he gave his only Son that whosoever believes in him should not perish but have eternal life." That is God's amazing grace, and that is the only way spiritual healing can happen.

In *Come Share the Being*, Bob Benson wrote about God's incredible grace and the amazing ways God shares himself with us:

> Do you remember when they had
> old fashioned Sunday school picnics?
> It was before air-conditioning.
> They said, "We'll meet at Sycamore Lodge
> in Shelby Park at 4:30 Saturday.
> You bring your supper and we'll furnish the tea."
>
> But you came home at the last minute
> and when you got ready
> to pack your lunch,
> all you could find in the refrigerator
> was one dried up piece of baloney
> and just enough mustard in the bottom of the jar
> so that you got it all over your knuckles
> trying to get to it.
> And there were just two stale pieces of bread.
> So you made your baloney sandwich
> and wrapped it in some brown bag
> and went to the picnic.
>
> And when it came time to eat
> you sat at the end of a table and spread
> out your sandwich.
> But the folks next to you—the lady was a good cook
> and she had worked all day
> and she had fried chicken, and baked beans,
> and potato salad, and homemade rolls,

and sliced tomatoes,
and pickles, and olives, and celery,
and topped it off with
two big homemade chocolate pies.
And they spread it all out beside you
and there you were with your baloney sandwich.

But they said to you,
"Why don't we put it all together?"
"No, I couldn't do that, I just couldn't even think of it,"
you murmured embarrassedly.
"Oh, come on, there's plenty of chicken
and plenty of pie, and plenty of everything—
and we just love baloney sandwiches.
Let's just put it all together."
And so you did and there you sat—
eating like a king
when you came like a pauper.

The point is obvious: We bring our little, and God brings his much, and in his amazing grace, God says, "Let's put it all together." If we will only accept it in faith, God has a banquet for us when we are hungry. God has healing for us when we are hurting. God can satisfy the hollow emptiness within us. God can make the wounded whole. God can heal the sin-sick soul. Through the power, the healing power of his love, God can bring healing where it hurts.